PACK YOUR
LUGGAGE
BUT LEAVE YOUR
BAGGAGE

PACK YOUR
LUGGAGE
BUT LEAVE YOUR
BAGGAGE

Practical Everyday Tips for
MEN AND WOMEN
to Help Get through This
Thing We Call Life!

Ethel Mae

ARCHWAY
PUBLISHING

Archway Publishing books may be ordered through booksellers or by contacting:

Archway Publishing
1663 Liberty Drive
Bloomington, IN 47403
www.archwaypublishing.com
1 (888) 242-5904

ISBN: 978-1-4808-8229-4 (sc)
ISBN: 978-1-4808-8230-0 (hc)
ISBN: 978-1-4808-8228-7 (e)

Library of Congress Control Number: 2019915807

Print information available on the last page.

Archway Publishing rev. date: 10/28/2019

"Consider that there is more to life than what you already know."

Contents

Acknowledgements

My mother, you are my number one fan and biggest supporter. We've come a long way baby!

Melanie Hamilton, founder of My 2nd Chance, your encouragement and vision is where the inspiration for the title came from.

Andree DaCosta, my sister-daughter, for being my unofficial editor, proofreader, and market research group.

I am grateful to God, the almighty creator of all things, for the gift of words.

To those who came and stayed, thank you! To those who came and left, thank you! To those who are yet to come, thank you!

I thank you!

Introduction

This book covers the important theme of self-love and self-improvement. We all have issues from our past that can haunt us in the present and if left without getting help and support will affect the future. We can embrace our past experiences and use them as stepping-stones to avoid pitfalls moving forward. We can use the lessons learnt throughout our lives with people who love, support and want to see us living our best most fulfilled life.

This book is filled with tips regarding how you can gain the strength to motivate yourself to look within and find self-love and self-acceptance. Self-love and self-acceptance, which translates to positivity and hope in other aspects of your life.

This book will help you to identify areas in your life that you are unhappy with and challenge you to take the step forward to make a change.

Your happiness is an inside job. It's waiting for you to make that step to let go of all you are holding on to that is keeping you back. That could be hurt, shame or guilt of the past through to being able to forgive those who have caused you pain in your life. The advice and encouragement through this book will help you on the road to being able to do that, to let it all go. It will help you to Pack Your Luggage, But Leave your Baggage".

Pack Light!

*Be careful of your
inner dialogue.
What you constantly
tell yourself about yourself
is what you will ultimately
end up believing
about yourself!*

~ Ethel Mae

I'm in Love..........
With Me!

Now, I don't mean in a conceited *"I love me and don't have room to love anyone else but me"* kind of way. I mean in the *"I am not perfect, I have flaws, I have a past, I may not have had the best start in life, and I mess up sometimes, but, I love me warts and all; I accept that I am not perfect, but I am trying to be the best me I can be. I will make mistakes in life, but I mean no one harm. I have hobbies, I have interests, I want to take care of myself and pursue things in life"*.

I ♡ ME

I 👂 ME

I Respect ME

And having someone to do those things with is a bonus, but don't neglect loving yourself, getting to know who you are, knowing your likes and dislikes trying to please someone else.

The sad truth is there are many people who do not know who they are at their core. They don't know the true essence of who they really are. There are also those who do not know what they like or dislike. Having spent so much time trying to get people to like them, they

1

end up trying to mirror those people with hopes that they will, in turn, think "we have things in common" and "we are so compatible." Especially in a relationship setting

But it is time to peel back the layers and really look at yourself; take a long deep look and ask, "Who am I?" "What do I like?" "What do I dislike?" "What do I want to do with my life?" "Where is my life heading?" It can even be something as simple as "what foods do I like to eat?" and What places do I like to go?"

Too often, we skip loving and looking into ourselves because we are too busy being all things to all people. We all are, to some extent, people pleasers, wanting to do things to please and help others. However, it is when you lose your identity trying to conform and fit into everyone else's mold that you gradually lose yourself.

Again, don't get me wrong, when you meet another person, especially one that you are interested in pursuing a relationship with, it is great to support and show interest in their likes and hobbies. The danger is in losing yourself by denying and hiding your likes and dislikes in an attempt to fit into what you think they want you to be.

Before you can truthfully answer those questions, you will need to find out the thing about you that you don't want to face or acknowledge. The reason why you would rather live someone else's life than get to know yourself? It could be your upbringing or your relationship with your family, or past relationships. It could be any number of experiences that have left a negative impact or a bad memory. There are things that happen in life that can leave a feeling of shame or embarrassment enough to make you want to hide certain parts of your life and cause you to live with a part of you buried deep. But regardless of what the cause is, it is not too late. It is not too late to get help, it is not too late to find you and fall in love with you.

I recall a time in my life when I was between relationships, I would sit at home watching movies, listening to music, and reading books. Basically, living the life of a recluse other than going to work. It wasn't until I got bored of my own company and fed up of feeling as though I was just existing that I took action and did something about it. I made the decision to learn who I was, and I learnt about me. I went to the movies by myself, I took myself out to restaurants, I took salsa lessons (and LOVED IT), I went to art galleries, and even went on vacation by myself, twice! I started to spend healthy time with me, getting to know me, what I liked, and things I wanted to do. Going as far as making a bucket list.

The more I learnt about myself, the more I realized that I wasn't so bad after all! I learnt that I didn't have to hide from my past, from those experiences. I realized that I didn't have to feel ashamed or embarrassed by anything I had been through. I learnt that I didn't have to deny who I was or what I liked. In short, I didn't have to hide me. You know why? Because the right people will like me and love me for me.

The right people will respect that yes, I have a past, yes, I make, have made and will continue to make mistakes, and I may not have the best background. The right people will love me for who I am, they will respect my likes and dislikes, they will support me in the things I like to do as I support them in theirs. The right people will also help me to accept me and be my biggest supporters as I reciprocate.

By learning about myself, I realized that I am quite funny, I LOVE seafood, and I learnt how to be happy with me. I didn't need a relationship to make me feel complete. I was a complete person entering into a union and we were then able to complement and be an asset to each other.

Until you can truly love and accept who you are, you will never really know how to love others. Until you know who you are, how will you know how to give of your real self to others? Until you know who you are, you won't know what you have within you that can be of benefit to others. You have so much goodness within you just waiting to be shared. You have so many life experiences that others can learn from and that can help others in their lives.

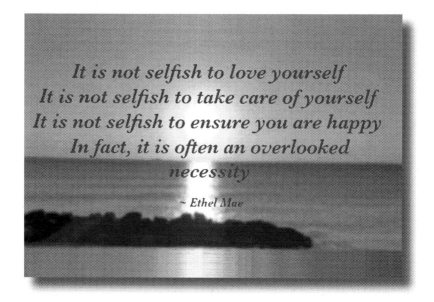

It is not selfish to love yourself
It is not selfish to take care of yourself
It is not selfish to ensure you are happy
In fact, it is often an overlooked
necessity

~ Ethel Mae

Your Thoughts.........

"Keep your individuality, keep your uniqueness, as that is what drew people to you in the first place! Keep learning about you, keep loving you! Your world will be more beautiful for it and you will make the world a more beautiful place for those who share it with you."

Dare to leave your comfort zone and reach beyond yourself.

~ Ethel Mae

Are You Sick & Tired of Being Sick & Tired?

You see, I know exactly what it's like to feel that way. At one time in my life, I was at the opposite end of the spectrum.

I woke up to the same boring routine day in, day out, every day was the same thing.

I've been broke and broken, been abused, felt abandoned by family and friends. I have been completely depressed, disillusioned, and frus-

Ups and downs in life are essential to keep us moving and growing. Lack of movement leads to stagnation, were nothing grows. No movement, a straight line means we are not alive, just check an E.C.G. machine!

~ Ethel Mae

trated with the state (yes, state) of my life, my relationships, my friendships, and my career for many, many years.

Making £12 an hour at work. After paying bills, I was broke all over again, there was a lot of month left at the end of the money. So, I got a second job and still broke! I felt as though my life had no purpose, no meaning, and that I was aimlessly just ambling through life.

My relationships had no substance and were based more on being physical than on love and trust. They were unfulfilling and unsatisfying and left me feeling even more lonely and disappointed than ever. Much of that disappointment was with myself. To be brutally honest, my life was a mess and I wasn't happy with my journey in life so far. I had lost my spark, I was just going through the motions of 'living.'

Have you ever stopped to wonder, "what am I doing?" Have you ever stopped to wonder, "is my life progressing?" Have you ever stopped to wonder, "where will my next meal come from?" Have you ever stopped to wonder, "where will the money to pay my bills come from?" Have you ever stopped to wonder, "is my relationship healthy, do they love me enough to support me no matter what?" Have you ever stopped to wonder, "why do I give so much and get so little in return?" Well, I have asked myself ALL of those questions at one point in my life and didn't like the answers that I came up with.

I 'tried'—or at least, I thought I did—everything I knew to change my life and experience more love and happiness. I got sick and tired of feeling like the Smokey Robinson song 'Tracks of my Tears.' I was tired of trying to hide from everyone and lying to myself about the pain, the hurt, the loneliness, the anger, the disappointments, the abuse. I was tired of all the things that came as the result of bad decisions that I had made, bad relationships I had been involved in, not investing wisely in my career, my finances, my life, and disappointments that I seemed to always carry with me like an invisible backpack. I remember sitting at home one day, checking my emails,

I don't recall where the email came from, but it was a book about positive thinking. I bought the book, the audio book, and the DVD, I completely immersed myself in it in the hope that all I would need to do is think positively. I've tried affirmations, I prayed, and I tried to still my mind by meditating. I went out and bought even more books on the law of attraction, positive thinking, and various self-help books.

I was willing to try almost anything, I wanted—no, I NEEDED—a better life. I saw other people happy, successful, and enjoying their life and I wanted that. I wanted to be happy, I wanted to be successful like they were, I wanted to shop and buy nice things without worrying about it or trying to justify spending money on a luxury rather than paying a bill.

I remember a few birthdays ago my mother sent me money as a gift, her instructions were "spend the money on yourself and don't use it to pay any bills". That is just how much I was living from hand to mouth. I wanted to be in a loving relationship with someone who truly loved ME, who respects ME. I knew it was all possible as I had seen others do it. I just didn't know what their secret to success was.

I still didn't feel like I was making much progress, with all of the books, CD's and DVD's I had gone through. You see, I didn't realize that I would actually have to DO something. I would need to work at changing. Things didn't work out the way I had hoped at first. Some of the things I tried were so confusing, while other methods were so out there.

Telling you that all you need to do is think positive thoughts and your life will change. OK, that's nice but...that didn't work! Seems like the more things I tried, the more confused I became about which tools to use to improve my life. Not only was I broke, I was in debt, and in a 'sort of' relationship. Things just progressively got worse and worse.

Many people don't know this but... I actually tried to take my own life. I had a bottle of 500 painkillers and decided I had had enough. I just wanted the pain to end. It's amazing that, at what seems to be the lowest point of your life, the fighter in you shows up and takes over.

After that incident, I knew I had to do something different. I just didn't know what. I knew I needed something that would really change the direction of the life and existence that I was experiencing. I was so low, but knew I had to keep going because there had to be something that would help change my life. There had to be more.

I decided right then that I was going to take charge and responsibility of my life. I wasn't going to live my life full of regrets, full of bitterness, broke and unfulfilled like i had been. I ended my 'sort of' relationship, I left my job, packed up all my worldly goods and went to stay with my mother in Florida. I took a few months out to get myself together. I know this is not an option for most people, it is just a part of the process that I went through. I knew I needed to take action, I couldn't just think up a better life, so I had to work at making a better life happen.

I had to take a good, long hard look at myself; I had to actually face myself. I had to be very open and honest with ME. I had to learn how to love ME, I had to learn to forgive ME, and in doing so, I had to LET GO of the things that were blocking me and holding me back. Things like unforgiveness, anger, and bitterness. Things I didn't really know until I took the time to go through a specific, detailed, and hard—but oh so achievable—process. I had to peel back the layers, wade through my stuff, look at myself and rebuild myself, from the ground up.

Are you ready to start living the life of your dreams? I am here to help you, but ultimately, the choice is yours.

Your Thoughts..........

Do Not Be CONFORMED, But Be TRANSFORMED

There is no progression in conforming, conforming lacks movement. However, to be transformed means that there is movement and progress. To be transformed means to make a thorough and dramatic change.

One way to do this is to change or renew your mind. You have to change how you think, change your view of life. You must have to CHANGE.

Choose today, will you CONFORM or TRANSFORM? Will you take courage and change, or will you stay the same?

It's a Cruise

Think of life as taking a cruise. Enjoy the moment, enjoy the journey, knowing that you are heading in the right direction towards your destination, towards achieving your goals. Don't be in too much of a rush that you don't enjoy arriving at the destination, as you'll miss the essence of the journey because you rushed through it, the journey is where the lessons are learnt.

Being on a cruise there is so much to do to occupy your time, to allow you to relax and enjoy the journey. Even though you are in a total state of relaxation and enjoyment, you have the confidence that you are on the right path and your arrival at a new place will be amazing, and you are sure of your arrival.

While cruising, take the time to look at and admire your surroundings, the scenery. Take the time to fully pay attention to how you are navigating your journey.

Don't fall into the temptation of wanting to rush through the journey. Don't be in a hurry to race through your experiences. Impatience only leads to frustration, frustration that you haven't reached your goals within a set timeframe, frustration that you may not be where you thought you would be in a set time frame.

Enjoy the moment, enjoy where you are now, recognize how far you have come, because this will allow you to appreciate the now and also the realization that progress is in fact being made. Yes, it is important to set a time for when you want to achieve the goals you have made. But sometimes, there are delays, life happens. During these times, don't be too hard on yourself, especially if the delay was beyond your control.

It is important to look back occasionally to see just how far you have come, to see how much you have achieved, to help spur you on, during the hard days. This will help when it comes to setting future goals with realistic targets.

Setting realistic targets is vital, it is being honest and open about what you can realistically do and by when. Be honest with the amount of time that you have for any project, be honest about your motivation to really get these goals achieved.

Maybe it's not that you didn't have enough time to get your goals achieved, but that these goals were not of enough importance for you to invest the time needed, or you procrastinated. Maybe you need to re-evaluate your goals and be honest about whether or not these are really for you, what are/were your reasons behind setting those particular goals? Never set goals based on what another person wants for you, another person's opinion of you, or because they told you that is what you should do. Set YOUR goals based on what YOU want for YOUR life and what YOU want from life.

If you are unable to reach any of your goals within the time for whatever reason, it should not be used to beat yourself up. Look at why the goals had not been achieved and address accordingly. Maybe the timeframe wasn't realistic to begin with or your motivation behind setting those goals wasn't correct.

But whatever you do, enjoy the journey, you will get to the destination at the right time and in the right frame of mind.

Your Thoughts..........

"Not just to be positioned among the best, but quietly reinvent the wheel, set the bar higher than anybody else has done before. Then go and smash that!"

Help Wanted...., Men Seeking Clarity for Life and for Love

For too long we have bought into the myth that, "a real man, this and a real man that." Ideals that put so much pressure on men to be at their "optimal peak" all the time, to be on top of their game in every circumstance. Which in all honesty is unfair and unrealistic.

There are a lot of men silently suffering from depression, hurt, being kept from being in their children's lives. Men wanting a family, the male biological clock ticking. Men silently screaming and dying inside. Feeling as though they are unable to express their pain, their fears, their heart because we now live in a world where "real men" don't do that! An age that will define a man by what he has and what he is supposed to be doing, rather than allowing men to have the luxury of seeking help to be clear on their path, their goals and their dreams. If we look carefully and listen, we can tell which men are the ones silently screaming and suffering.

From an early age boys are told to "boys don't cry, man up, stop whining, toughen up, get over it, pick yourself up by your bootstraps" and quite a few more clichés. Boys are taught to celebrate their wins and never mention their losses. Men are strong, emotions are for the weak is what society would have us believe. We are told that vulnerability is a sign of weakness and makes a man less of a protector and a provider if they dare to show any emotion. Nothing could actually be further from the truth.

Feelings and emotions are evidence that you are human and is a sign of good mental and emotional health. There is no shame in expressing emotions. Men should not be forced to wear a tough guy mask to prove their masculinity. By wearing the mask many are far from who they are pretending to be. This blocks men from being and feeling their own humanity. This results in risking alienation should men dare to allow themselves to feel. By not allowing themselves to give in to emotions, can lead in many cases to feelings of unexpressed isolation. This repression of emotions causes untold and unnecessary suffering and mental health issues for men in all walks of life.

Emotions are part of what make us all real people. Having the chance to feel and express themselves when it comes to being able to grieve a loss, express regret, feel fear or happiness, men are told that feelings are for girls or sissies. That any emotions that looks remotely like, sadness, love, regret, pain, fear or uncertainty are not an experience men should ever even contemplate having. It supposedly puts their masculinity into question.

It shouldn't have to be the case that men must bury, hide or not have any emotions. This is basically saying that you either have feelings and emotions or bury that away and stop being a person. It shouldn't be either or in order to be a man. The reality is men, *real men*, are allowed to feel anger, pain, love and are at times detached. Those emotions are a perfectly accepted interpretation of masculinity.

What men do need is the very thing they fear. And left unchecked and in denial of being emotionally honest, the results have deep rooted, and harmful consequences.

Life and love happens to us all sooner or later. From our first crush, first job, marriage, children, life is waiting for us.

When going through challenges women are encouraged to seek help, express her feelings or talk it through, to work through and process and their feelings. A man on the other hand will be openly belittled for the exact same things.

A man who dares to open up, share and express too much of what he is going through is called or labeled a "whiny little bitch" or "pussy-whipped" or worse. And God forbid a man actually cries. As though crying is the biggest cardinal sin that a man can commit emotionally.

Crying is like a cleansing; this cleansing is therapeutic, it releases pent up stress and frustration which then allows for clearer thinking. The silent internal screaming that needs a release. Men cry too...., and that's a good thing.

By refusing to acknowledge that men have emotional needs and emotions makes it difficult for men to give and receive emotional support. As a result, men who admit to any feeling outside of the narrow range, of feelings acceptable for a man, namely anger are subjected to ridicule instead of being given much needed supported.

By supporting and encouraging men to embrace their emotional health would hugely benefit their families. Why we continue to limit the emotional health of men when it serves no one, is quite frankly an archaic ideal, which leads to poor mental health.

It is well known that men are significantly less likely to use mental health services in comparison to women. This is especially so for Black, Latino, Indian and Asian men, who have a much lower rate of using these services than their white counterparts, and women in general. Men are more likely to brush it off as fatigue, irritability or a general lack of interest rather than be honest and admit to needing help. In other words, men are much more likely to suffer in silence, sadly, especially minority men.

This is often brushed off as, him being stubborn and stems from age old perceptions and interpretations that focus on and highlight the "tough guy, bravado" definitions of masculinity.

What are the alternatives of ignoring the emotional and mental health of men? Stress-induced heart attacks, overindulging in alcohol, and a host of other health and mental health issues. Although, these are extreme examples, however, there are the often more subtle overlooked forms of damage, loneliness, lack of communication in relationships, fear, depression, bottled-up pain, loss, extreme detachment and regret. The often harder to see effects that men fight to remain hidden.

How can we help men to get past the butch masculine stereotypes? We as a society we can stop buying into the "real men do this" and "real men do that" hype. That really helps no one, it only succeeds in at times making men actually feel inadequate.

We give men space and time for self-care. Start with simple things like manicures, pedicures and generally taking the time to look after themselves, more than the regular haircut. It is past due to break away from those types of negatives that surround masculinity fueled by beliefs in rigid standards that suggest self-care is only for women.

It is time that the silent screams and internal cries of men are no longer silenced but given the consideration that they are literally dying for.

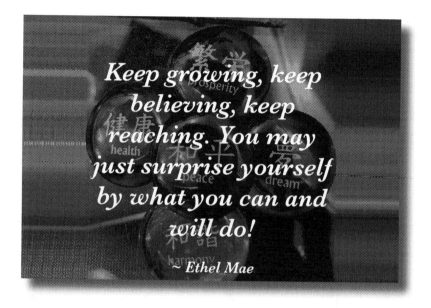

Keep growing, keep believing, keep reaching. You may just surprise yourself by what you can and will do!

~ Ethel Mae

Your Thoughts.........

"It is a lesson we all should learn.
To try, and try, and try again

Don't fret if we don't succeed
at the first turn, Still try,
and try, and try again!"

Dragging

There are a lot of people pulling/dragging a lot of stuff behind them.

On a recent road trip where I was fortunate for once to be the passenger, I noticed a lot of vehicles that were pulling or towing something behind them. Trailers, boats etc. It made me think about it in terms of life, how many of us have things hitched to us that we are literally pulling/dragging something behind us?

Look at a laden down vehicle, pulling an extra load. To move it uses more gas and makes the vehicle heavier and harder to maneuver. Isn't that what all of the extra baggage we walk around with daily is doing to us? Making us use up extra energy and making us tired? Tired mentally, emotionally, physically, and spiritually.

What will it take for you to lay all of it down and be free of all the past hurts, fears, disappointments?

What will it take for you to cut loose, and lay it all down, and get rid of it once and for all? No picking your stuff back up and hitching it to yourself for the next 'trip.'

Isn't today a good day to start?

Your Thoughts..........

_____

_____

_____

_____

_____

_____

_____

_____

_____

_____

_____

_____

_____

"There are different types of people in the world, those who tell you that you cannot make a difference, there are those who are afraid to try and those who are afraid you will succeed. There are different kinds of people in the world, the ones that suck the life out of every day, and the ones that let every day suck the life out of them. And then there are the types of people in this world who face each day with hope and believe that this will be their best day yet filled with limitless possibilities."

Confront It, To Overcome It

Have you ever wondered why the same things keep happening in your life over and over and over again? The same pattern, time after time after time?

What we don't deal with and fix will keep repeating itself in your life until the lesson is learnt.

In short "what you don't repair, you will keep on repeating." You are destined to keep repeating the same mistakes until you learn the lesson.

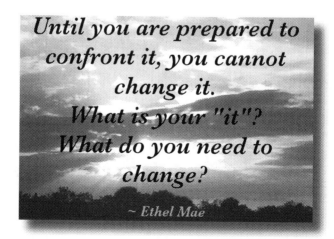

Until you are prepared to confront it, you cannot change it.
What is your "it"?
What do you need to change?

~ Ethel Mae

The things you confront, you are able to overcome.

In other words, what you do not confront, you cannot overcome.

Powerful words indeed.

In order to make a real change, you must first identify the areas within that need to or you would like to change, then take action.

It will be hard work, but the results and the reward will be immeasurable.

Think about it!

Each Day is a New Day

Things that happened yesterday are over, done, they are gone. The trouble is we play it over and over again in our minds. All the events of yesterday are finished and gone, and only stay alive in your mind for as long as you allow them, for as long as you keep replaying them.

Today is a new day full of new possibilities, new hopes, and new dreams. Today is a new beginning.

Think on that for a while, let it really sink in. Replace the negative recordings of all your yesterdays and write the script with all your hopes for tomorrow.

"Each day is a new day."

Your Thoughts.........

_____

_____

_____

_____

_____

_____

_____

_____

_____

_____

_____

_____

Kintsugi - Gold Repair

Be careful of your inner dialogue, what you constantly tell yourself about yourself, is what you will ultimately end up believing about yourself!

You are who you've been looking for! "Your capacity to love others is limited only by your capacity to love yourself."

How often are you quick to jump to the defense of those you love and care about, to then only beat yourself up and berate yourself. How often have you heard someone speak negatively about themselves and get upset with them for doing so? Then say something negative or derogatory to or about yourself "I'm so -----------" (fill in the blank). Speak well of yourself and speak well to yourself. Speak life into yourself and into others.

None of us are perfect. We are all beautifully broken, we are all beautifully flawed, each in our own unique and beautiful way.

In Japan, broken objects are often repaired with gold. The flaw is then seen as a unique piece of the objects history which adds to its beauty and value.

Even the bible says, "love your neighbor as YOURSELF". Therefore, love of yourself is a MUST for you to even begin to love others.

So again, be careful of your inner dialogue, what you constantly tell yourself about yourself, is what you will ultimately end up believing about yourself! Because ultimately we are all beautifully broken.

Nothing is Ever a Waste.

Nothing is ever a waste. No experience, hurt, struggle, or dream is ever a waste.

If you feel as though you have wasted years of your life in the wrong job, spending time with the wrong people, making the wrong choices, or not doing anything at all, It is not too late. It's not too late to change the channel, to make a fresh start.

The only time experiences are a "waste" is if no lesson is learnt from the experience, no lesson is learnt from the pain, or the struggle.

You can start today to turn your life and situation around. By learning from your past, you will emerge a stronger, wiser, and better person than you ever were before. You can start today to launch into your destiny.

All things are possible if you just believe. And remember that nothing is ever a waste!

Your Thoughts..........

If You Despise Your Dream, You Delay Your Future

If you have a dream or a vision, do not think all is lost because "it's just a dream." That just means it is now time to put some FOUNDATIONS under your dreams and work towards making them a reality.

But don't stop dreaming big, don't stop believing or having faith. Believe that you can have a better life, keep working towards that dreams, you WILL get there, you will make it.

I dare you to dream big, it won't cost you anything. There is no invoice waiting for you when wake up from dreaming.

Don't believe me? Try it and see!

So, dream on and DREAM BIG.

We are faced with two choices
every day.
Stay asleep and dream or get up,
chase those dreams.
Make them happen!

~ Ethel Mae

Why Worry? Who by Worrying Can Add a Single Second to Their Life?

The dictionary definition of worry is to give way to anxiety or unease; allow one's mind to dwell on difficulty or troubles. To fret, be concerned, be anxious, agonize, overthink, brood, panic, lose sleep, get worked up, get stressed, get in a state, stew, torment oneself.

Imagine if all of the energy and exertion it takes to worry was turned on its head and used to think about, meditate on, and visualize positive outcomes. If all of that time effort and energy was put into working towards making things happen to achieve your goals, to making positive changes and taking bold steps.

I'll tell you what would happen, you would be an unstoppable force to be reckoned with. You would be a powerhouse of possibilities and positivity.

If you know how to worry, you know how to meditate. It takes the same level of energy to do both. Worry is just a negative form of meditation. By worrying you are meditating on all the worst-case scenarios.

So why worry?

Your Thoughts.........

_____

_____

_____

_____

_____

_____

_____

_____

_____

_____

_____

_____

_____

_____

You Are Responsible!

Only you are responsible for what you do, think, and feel. You can choose to hold on to painful events, like a weight around your neck, or you can choose to remove that burden by releasing it (giving it no more emotional or mental energy, thus taking away its power) and living a happier life, despite past or current circumstances.

In other words, let the past be in the past, and live in the moment, live for right now. You can't change what happened in the past, but you have a choice over how you live now and how you live moving forward.

You are responsible for what you do, think, and feel. You are responsible for forgiving others, and most importantly you are responsible for forgiving yourself.

Forgiveness is about releasing your negative emotions and perceptions about painful events. Otherwise, you keep yourself chained to those events or people—you keep it alive within you—and you carry it with you wherever you go. It is a very heavy burden to carry around and you end up crippling yourself emotionally, mentally, spiritually, and physically.

Holding on to anger, resentment, etc. keeps you in a 'victim' mode—a powerless state. It means you are letting the people who have hurt you in the past dictate who you are in the present moment and in the future. You can take your power back by releasing those negative emotions and no longer letting them have control over your thoughts, feelings, and actions. Because ultimately, what angers you controls you.

It's time to stop letting the past control you, it's time to stop allowing the past to hold you captive. It's time to break free because, *you* are responsible.

Your Thoughts..........

Move

Without movement, how do we measure our growth? Without the lows, how can we appreciate the highs? Without the dark how can we appreciate the light? Without rain we wouldn't have rainbows.

To fully live, we must understand that highs, lows, sunshine, and rain are all necessary. Live in the sunshine, learn to dance in the rain, and grow through life.

Keep moving, growing and stretching.
Keep setting and achieving your goals.
There is no creativity in stillness.
The only thing that has an income from being still is a parking meter.

~ Ethel Mae

The Man/Woman in The Mirror

To be able to recognize something, you must know it.

You know a rose when you see one, you know rain when you see, hear and feel it, the list could go on and on.

The good you see and find in others is within you too.

The faults you see and find in others are within you too.

The possibilities you see in others are possible for you to.

The beauty of life and nature you see around you, is your beauty.

The world around you, the circle in which you dwell, the influences in your life are a reflection; a mirror showing you the person you are.

What you see and either like or dislike in others, shows you what you like or dislike within yourself.

Always see the best in others, and you will always be your best.

Give to others and you give to yourself.

Be patient with others, allowing them the time and space they need to grow; to grow in their own time, in their own space, in their own way, and not in your set time frame, as what may be good, necessary, or relevant for your life may not be the same for another. But rather be there to encourage, be there to support, be there to help guide. Do not be quick to give up on people or discard them when they are not conforming to your schedule, as I am sure they would not give up on you as easily.

Appreciate beauty and what is beautiful, and you will be beautiful.

Respect and admire creativity, and you will be creative.

Love unconditionally, give love, show love, be love, and you will be loved.

Seek to understand and appreciate that everyone has a path, a journey, a story, and you will be understood.

Take the time to listen, and your voice will be heard.

Teach, and you will learn.

Show your best you to the person in the mirror and you'll be happy with the person looking back at you.

Think and meditate on whatever qualities you would like to have and believe that you are achieving them; believe that you are them.

Find qualities that you would like to exude; gratitude, love, health, wisdom, a positive spirit and attitude, being nonjudgmental of yourself or others, discernment, the strength and power for good deeds and success, etc.

Fill your mind with the thought of achieving these qualities; that you are making things happen.

The more you strive to make this happen, the more you will notice you are changing, you are becoming these qualities, you will start to see a new person in the mirror; you will have peace. The more you practice and meditate on this, the more persistent and patient you are. You will become conscious and find life growing more beautiful to you; your strength will be increased in all areas of your life, physically, spiritually, and emotionally.

To change your world, the change must first come from within you.

To blame, point the finger, and complain will only make matters worse, as you are ultimately looking without and not looking within.

Whatever you care about is your responsibility to cherish and keep.

Your Thoughts.........

_____

_____

_____

_____

_____

_____

_____

_____

_____

_____

_____

_____

"Your TEST will become your TESTimony, what you GO through, you GROW through. Don't stop dreaming and pushing forward towards your dreams and your goals. Many do not have the best start in life, it is not about where or how you start; that could be with addictions, abuse, neglect, or being abandoned. This is the reality of what many people go through."

"What you hate, you become.
But what you forgive, you
are released from."

It's always better to live in love, joy, and peace. The fruits of the spirit.

Remember to forget to be unforgiving.

Remember to forget to hold grudges.

Remember to forget being resentful.

Remember to forget to hate

Remember love and have an open heart.

By being unforgiving and resentful, you are assisting and drawing negativity rather than resisting it.

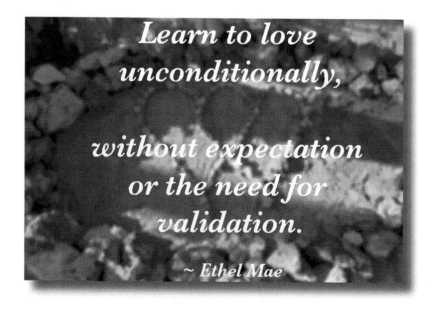

Learn to love unconditionally,

without expectation or the need for validation.

~ Ethel Mae

Your Thoughts..........

It's Time You Remembered Who You Are

You are not your job, your children, your house, or your bank account. You are not your activities, your worries or the labels other people give you. You are not a statistic or a number. These are titles; it is what you do, not who you are.

Like an actor, you play these roles, and like a good actor, you sometimes forget who you really are underneath all of the titles you have.

Time to wake up and remember that you are a being of immense power and breathtaking beauty created in the image of God. You are creative, ever evolving, slowly unravelling and developing.

You are love, you are loved.

Love that goes beyond the physical and touches you at your core, from deep within.

> *I want my life, my journey, my story to be such an example and an inspiration, that others will look on and be encouraged to keep going.*
>
> *~ Ethel Mae*

You have peace, you *are* peace, a being of true unshakeable tranquility.

You are all of these and so much more.

Time to breathe, be still, and Time to remind yourself.

Time to remember who you are!

Your Thoughts..........

Behind the Mask
The Me Hidden
from All

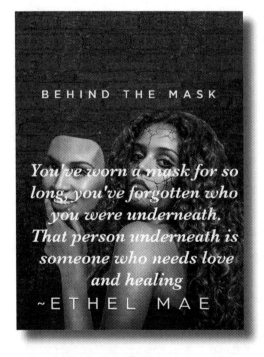

BEHIND THE MASK

You've worn a mask for so long, you've forgotten who you were underneath. That person underneath is someone who needs love and healing

~ETHEL MAE

What happens when you have a second, third, or even fourth you? What happens when you KNOW that you have different sides to you that you have NEVER let anyone else see? You hide your spirituality, you hide your culture, you hide your past, you hide your pain. In general, you hide your true personality, your true self.

This is usually a result of fear, lack of confidence, or insecurity, and in extreme cases, all of the above. A fear of what other people may think of your beliefs or the culture you were born into. Fear of what people may think of the things you have done in your past or what was done to you.

This makes you feel insecure or lack confidence in yourself and the need to passively please other people at your expense. The problem with this is that it leads to you never being truly happy, it leads to you being nervous or anxious when certain topics of conversation are brought up.

You may also be seen as shy, quiet an introvert. All along, you are just trying to blend into the background so that you do not draw attention to yourself in the hope that no one will ask you a question about YOU or what you think.

You may be at the opposite end of the spectrum, being the comedian, or an extrovert. Hiding behind that to appear as though you have it altogether so no one would think you had a mask in place, that you are in actual fact hiding.

It may stem from an early age in your life when you expressed an opinion and were cruelly made fun of or made to feel like your beliefs, culture, or opinion was weird, odd or not the norm. Or someone made you feel as though you are stupid (which you are not!) With this, you learnt to not speak up or to second guess and question yourself and the validity of what you have to share.

I spoke to a person who told me that as a child, they were always told to be quiet whenever they asked a question. So, guess what happened to them? They learnt to not speak, this led to years of passive aggressive behavior, years of not being able to make or keep friends. Simply put, years of being frustrated, bitter, and angry. Until they made a friend who noticed this and was patient enough to help guide them through the process of dropping the mask and breaking free.

"All it takes to hide is a beautifully fake smile so no one will see how broken you really are inside. You wear a mask for long enough hoping to forget who you really are, wholly broken into beautiful pieces."

This feeling of having to hide your inner self often leads to isolation, pain, and loneliness, and you not only hide your inner self but also begin to physically hide. You hide by making excuses why you can't go out when invited. You hide by not answering the phone when it rings; if you speak with no one, you will not say the 'wrong' thing. You hide by avoiding 'difficult' conversations that you believe may lead to you having to express an opinion. It leads to you almost being a 'nodding Nancy' just nodding and smiling when in a group setting. It is used as a defense mechanism because if people do not know you, they can't hurt you. So, your mask is your defense, your protective cloak.

Have you ever stopped to assess yourself physically without criticism? How is your posture when you walk or when you sit? Do you slouch or walk/sit tall? These are indicators to what you think about yourself. Are you trying to be inconspicuous or are you staring the world in the eye, ready to take on any challenge? If you are that person hiding behind the mask, you have learnt to not be present in the moment, and in doing so, all of your thoughts are focused on you and your inner turmoil, being totally aware of your presence.

How do we Overcome Hiding Behind These Masks?

The first step in overcoming this to take some time to self-reflect and go back in your life. Go back as far as you need to and look at why you believe what you believe; go back to what you believe may have occurred in your life that, for all intents and purposes, 'shut you up and shut you down'!

Once you have been able to do this, you need to forgive all of the people who played a part in your shut down. You will also need to forgive yourself for believing that you were not enough. It may take you having to confront some people. In some cases, it may be that you just have to let things go as the person may have passed away before you come to the point in your life that you are ready and able to forgive. But forgive you must!

Too many times we are waiting for an apology before we forgive. But in order to fully heal, so that you can take the mask off, it may mean forgiving people who are not sorry. For your own sanity you must forgive and let go. You will never forget, after all, you are human, but you must forgive.

The next step is to practice, practice, practice! Start by looking at yourself in the mirror with a smile on your face, shoulders back and head held high. Tell yourself how wonderful you are, how talented you are, how beautiful you are. Tell yourself you are going to have a wonderful day, a wonderful week, a wonderful month, a wonderful life, and any other positive things you can think of. I know this sounds really cheesy, but it works, it really does.

Try it and see, you may feel silly at first, but you will get past that. It helps in giving you that first boost of confidence to be able to express your true self honestly without feeling like you have to stop and be careful of everything you say.

Through a much deeper awareness of who you are, of your actions, and your thoughts about yourself, you can successfully retrain the way you think about yourself. This helps in the process of being able to come from behind the mask and it brings with it a feeling of absolute peace, freedom and lightness.

I'm not one of these coaches that will let you know 'you can do it, you just have to change your thoughts' and "poof" you are changed, or by speaking to yourself in the mirror, you will automatically overcome all of the limiting beliefs you have carried with you for years.

This takes work, real work, and is not for the faint hearted. It is for people who truly want to live a more fulfilled life, being able to communicate and socialize without fear or insecurity. With it comes a new awareness as to why you feel the way you do about yourself and how you communicate. It will also help you to know why you behave in a certain way when the spotlight is on you. It will help you develop the power of your voice, your posture, your body language, and the ability to deliver a clear and concise message with confidence and enthusiasm.

Once you get comfortable with who you are, this will go a long way to determine who you are capable of being. This new you should be the same person to show up in all life situations, instead of one of the many masks you wear depending on what situation or environment you are in. The goal is for you to be genuine, true, real, and consistent.

I truly do believe, from my years of experience, that everyone who wants to make a change in their lives either for the good or bad can do it. This is achieved by coaching, by surrounding yourself with people who are supportive and encouraging, who want you to succeed, and who will help you get there. People that make you feel safe and secure. And most importantly you doing the necessary work.

Many people cannot do this by themselves and this is where coaching comes in. Coaching can help achieve this, as it includes an understanding of a person, their history, their current situation and where they desire to be. The above, teamed together with your desire to succeed, makes it completely possible for you to go from behind the mask to having no mask. It will take you from being scared, nervous, and timid to truly amazing and powerful.

Remember ~ "When you wear a mask you are not your true self."

Everyone has baggage.
The blessing is having
people in your life
who love you enough
to help you unpack.

~ Ethel Mae

Your Thoughts..........

_____

_____

_____

_____

_____

_____

_____

_____

_____

_____

_____

Change Requires Work

Have you ever wondered why some people never change? Have you ever wondered why you cannot/don't change? Well, that is because change requires work.

Let's look at it from another perspective. For instance, if you wet yourself (extreme example, I know) initially it's warm and you sit in it. It gets cold for a while, but you block out the discomfort. You eventually become comfortable sitting in it, and it dries. You get used to the smell, you ignore the stain that has now been made, because you are comfortable, and it is familiar.

But the moment you decide you no longer want to sit in this condition is when the work begins. You have to first recognize the need to change. You then have to get up, take the soiled clothes off, wash yourself, and change your clothes. These may be simple actions, but it is change, nonetheless.

"The truth is rejected by many Because it is uncomfortable The truth will shake you to the very core of you, shake you to your foundation.

The truth requires change, When you stand in, and face your truth, Then and only then will your growth truly begin."

Many do not change because of the fear of leaving the familiar, or because they have become so comfortable with their condition that they don't even realize there is a need to change. There are those who think the problem is with everyone else. They are either always right or always the victim, or both. Some even go as far as recognizing the need to change but over think it so much they think themselves out of making the change.

But in life, everything has to change or else it will die. You are not the person you were seven years ago. Your hair, your nails, your skin have all changed over the space of seven years. Everything moves, everything grows; if it doesn't, it becomes stale, stagnant, and stinks. That manifests itself in people as bitterness, envy, jealousy sickness, and unforgiveness.

**Keep moving, keep changing, as that
is the only way you will grow.**

Because Change Requires Work!

Too often, we reject the truth because it is painful. The truth will make you face hard, real facts. Facing the truth, owning and standing in your truth requires work and change. It is only then, you will begin to grow.

Change requires work and actions speak much louder than words. It is very easy to agree that change needs to take place. Don't just SAY you have changed, SHOW that you have changed. As Gandhi put it, be the change you want to see in this world.

"Fear of change, is also fear progress"

66

Your Thoughts..........

_____

_____

_____

_____

_____

_____

_____

_____

_____

_____

_____

_____

Life doesn't necessarily give you what you deserve, it gives you what you fight for.

~ Ethel Mae

Attitude Adjustment
Keep it 100

Recently, I read something very interesting that really got me thinking.

If:
A B C D E F G H I J K L M N O P Q R S T U V W X Y Z
Is equal to;
1 2 3 4 5 6 7 8 9 10 11 12 13 14 15 16 17 18 19 20 21 22 23 24 25 26

That means
H+A+R+D+W+O+R+K;
8+1+18+4+23+15+18+11 = 98%

K+N+O+W+L+E+D+G+E;
11+14+15+23+12+5+4+7+5 = 96%

L+O+V+E;
12+15+22+5 = 54%

L+U+C+K;
12+21+3+11 = 47%

But none of the above add up to make 100%.

So, what does make 100%?

Is it Money?
M+O+N+E+Y
13+15+14+5+25 = 72%

Leadership?
L+E+A+D+E+R+S+H+I+P
12+5+1+4+5+18+19+8+9+16 = 97%

Every problem has a solution, only if we perhaps change our "ATTITUDE";

A+T+T+I+T+U+D+E;
1+20+20+9+20+21+4+5 = 100%

It is therefore OUR ATTITUDE towards Life and Work that makes OUR Life 100% Successful.

There are many different types of attitudes, a few examples are;

Optimism, Pessimism
Confident, Interest
Independent, Jealous
Courteous, Cooperative
Considerate, Inferior
Happy, Respectful
Authoritative, Sincere
Persistent, Honest
Sympathetic, Realistic
Faithful, Decisive

Trusting, Thoughtful
Determined, Loving
Hostile, Modest
Reliable, Tolerant
Humble, Cautious
Sarcastic, Helping
Hard Working

Some are positive attitudes, while others, well, not so much. But all is not lost if you have a healthy mixture of positive and negative, that makes you a real person. What causes the dysfunction and difficulties is when the negative traits outweigh or are more persistent than the positive.

Attitude is a way of thinking or feeling about someone or something, typically one that is reflected in behavior. What you think, what you do, and what you feel is what forms your attitude. While sometimes, knowledge and experience form our attitude, on other occasions, it is based on our assumptions and beliefs

Ask yourself, "what is my attitude? Is it positive? Can I see more good in it than bad, or is it an unbalanced amount of negativity?" If you are a positive, the-glass-is-half-full-kind of person, then great, keep doing what you're doing and don't forget to help someone else along this journey of life. Keep doing *that*!

However, if your attitude is more pessimistic and negative, a few (or a lot of) adjustments may be in order. Take a look at your attitude, write down your beliefs and the things that you believe are causing you to behave the way you do. Be honest with yourself when writing them down, especially if you really want to change your attitude and make the necessary adjustments.

Now writing the cold hard truth will be uncomfortable, and an eye opener as it may reveal things about yourself you would rather not admit to. But remember "the worst lies we tell, are the lies we tell ourselves." We all at times live in denial of our true selves, of who we are, what we think and even what we do. But if you are serious about making the adjustment, this is what you must go through, this is what it takes.

It takes for you to pull the band-aid off, expose the wound, get the right treatment to it and allow the healing to take place. While the wound is healing, it feels sore, it gets a little itchy, but these are all good signs that the skin is growing back in place to cover the wound. Once the wound has healed, it may leave a scar, but you will not forget that wound, you will remember what caused it, what the treatment was, and the healing process; basically what you had to do to get better.

It's the same with adjusting your attitude, write down the real 'ugly' truth about who you really are. What you can do to make the change, and what help you need. Yes, if you need help, make sure you get the right help. You may have to go outside of your circle in order to get the right help. Therapy, counselling whatever you have to do, "Just Do It!" Get yourself a coach or an accountability partner that will help you through the process and in doing so, success will naturally happen

Do you need an attitude adjustment?

Keep it

Your Thoughts..........

_____

_____

_____

_____

_____

_____

_____

_____

_____

_____

_____

_____

_____

Today...

Today, when I awoke, and gave thanks for another day and suddenly realized, that this is the best day of my life, ever! There were times when I wondered if I would

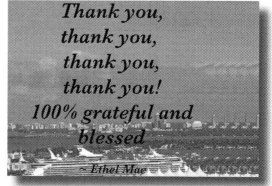

Thank you, thank you, thank you, thank you! 100% grateful and blessed

~ Ethel Mae

make it to today, times I thought I wouldn't make it to today, but I did!

And because of that, I will be grateful, appreciate all I have, and celebrate! Celebrate the battles won and those lost, celebrate all the good and pleasant things that have blessed my life and all that is still to come.

Today, I'm going to celebrate what an unbelievable life lived so far and the unbelievable life that still is yet to come. The accomplishments, the many blessings, yes, even the hardships, losses and difficult times, because they have served to make me stronger. They have served to give me wisdom, they have even served to make me more compassionate and passionate.

I will go through this day with my head held high, with a happy, grateful, and joyous heart. I will marvel at God's seemingly simple gifts: the morning dew, the sun, the clouds, the trees, the flowers, the birds, and the wonder and splendor of nature. Today, none of these miraculous creations will escape my notice.

Today, I will share my excitement and zeal for life with others. I'll make someone smile. I'll go out of my way to perform an unexpected act of kindness towards someone I don't even know.

Today, I'll give a heartfelt and sincere compliment to someone who seems down. I'll tell a child how special they are—after all, the children are the future and we must nurture and nourish them—and I'll tell someone I love just how much I care for them and how much they mean to me.

Today is the day I no longer worry about what I don't have and start being truly grateful for all the wonderful things God has already given me, as I know there is so much more on the way. The latter years will be greater than the former years.

I'll remember that to worry is just a waste of time because my faith in God's Divine Plan ensures everything will be just fine and will work out for my good. It always has and always will.

And tonight, before I go to bed, I'll raise my eyes to the heavens. I will give My Almighty Creator thanks and stand in awe at the beauty and wonder of the stars, the moon and all that is around me.

As the day ends and I lay my head down on my pillow, I will thank God for allowing me to have the best day of my life and I will mean it. I will sleep the sleep of a happy, contented child, full of excitement and expectation because now I know that tomorrow is going to be the best day of my life, ever!

And I am forever grateful.

Your Thoughts..........

_____

_____

_____

_____

_____

_____

_____

_____

_____

_____

_____

_____

_____

Your Words Have Power, Use Them Wisely

Your words have the power to heal a heart and wound a soul

Your words have the power to move others to tears and bring immense joy

Your words have the power to open a mind and shut down the freedom to speak

Your words have the power to create new worlds and kill a dream

Your words have the power to encourage and to delay

Your words have the power to build and to destroy

Your words have power, use them wisely.

In the words of Frederick Douglass "it is easier to build up a child than repair an adult." Your words and actions have power in your life and the life of others, use them wisely. Whenever you speak, you are actually prophesying your future.

So, speak life, speak health, speak wealth, speak all of the things you want to see and manifest in your life.

> *Death and life are in the power of the tongue,*
> *And those who love it will eat its fruit.*
> *~ Proverbs 18:21*

Your Thoughts..........

Happy New Year, Happy New You!

Happy New Year to you. No, I don't mean the December 31st at 11:59pm kind of Happy New Year. I mean the day, hour, or minute that you decide, I am going to start my life, I am going to do things differently. We look forward to the strike of midnight on January 1st to say "New Year, New Start" as though we are only given an opportunity for a new start once a year.

You are given 365 new chances each year, it's called a new day! With each new day you are given, you should let go of the mistakes, hurts, and stresses of yesterday, embrace the NEW fresh day with FRESH HOPE, FRESH FAITH, FRESH OPTIMISM, looking ahead, and moving forward. Do right. Do your best. Treat others as you want to be treated.

> *"I have mostly been impressed with the urgency*
> *of doing. Knowing is not enough, we must apply.*
> *Being willing is not enough, we must do."*
> *~ Leonardo da Vinci*

May the year ahead of you, be the year that all that is divinely ordained to be yours come to pass and manifest. May you leave the past in the past and celebrate life and living.

Old things have passed away; behold, all
things have become new.
~ 2 Corinthians 5:17

Many started and were not fortunate to see the end of the day. But you have been blessed with life, you made it through another day, so, give thanks and celebrate life and all that is to come. This WILL be the day, the year of manifestation, as everything you have worked for, everything your heart desires and everything God has promised WILL come to pass. I am praying for blessing for you as your purpose and His will for your life unfolds.

Dear God,

I am choosing to move into the "New Year" EMPTY and FREE of yesterday, of the past. I thank you for my accomplishments. I thank you for my triumphs. I thank you for my growth. I thank you for every single beautiful moment and memory that was created in my life, of which there have been many.

I also thank you for the moments and memories that weren't so great, that have been many of those too.

Dear God, I bless my past. I bless those in my past. I forgive every single person who has ever brought pain or discomfort into my life. Help me to continually walk and operate in forgiveness and remove all hidden unforgiveness that I may not even be aware of. As I know there was a lesson for ME in that encounter. I pray that I learned the lesson. If I didn't, TEACH ME in this instant so that I do not have to repeat the pain in the coming year, or ever.

I speak INCREASE in all areas of my life. I ask for a greater capacity to LOVE, to UNDERSTAND, to WORK, to CREATE, to FORGIVE, to LEAD, to PROSPER, to do YOUR WORK, and to be a contribution to Your Kingdom and the world.

I SURRENDER my entire life to you. To do whatever is in your will for my life. USE ME to help others. USE ME to heal others. USE ME to inspire others. USE ME to teach others. USE ME to make others happy. USE ME to love others. USE ME to give to others. USE ME to uplift others. USE ME to cherish others. USE ME to create with others. USE ME in whatever way you see fit for me.

I let go of what I WANT, and I ask that you give me the desires that YOU WANT for me.

I ask, Dear God, that you RENEW MY MIND. Give me a new way of thinking. Give me the knowledge and wisdom that I need to elevate my life and my way of operating. I surrender my old way of thinking, beliefs and habits that no longer serve You or my good. I surrender my thoughts of lack and limitation. I surrender my judgments. I choose to see PAST my obstacles, and I look to YOU to show me the way.

Dear God, I BOLDLY DECLARE that I am trusting you with all of my heart, with all of mind, with all of my soul and I stand in EXPECTATION of a MIRACULOUS year ahead AND BEYOND.

In your Divine Holy Name...

AMEN.

Your Thoughts..........

_____

_____

_____

_____

_____

_____

_____

_____

_____

_____

_____

_____

"Every Enemy Has a Predictable Pattern ..."

...except bats. They just move whatever way they please."

Every enemy has a predictable pattern...

...except bats. They just move whatever way they please.

This was the subject of a video game discussion board.

A lot of things that you may struggle with—your flaws, your insecurities, your issues—are all things you have battled with before.

Each day tell yourself:
Today is my day
All things are working
for my good
I am a winner
Good is with me
and in me
I am better today
than I was yesterday.

~ Ethel Mae

It is all too familiar; there is nothing new.

There is nothing new under the sun,
~ Ecclesiastes 1:9.

When you think about it, the battles and the struggles you have now, are what plagued you in previous years. Can you think of a single new issue that you have.

Many of the character flaws and behavior that you have wanted to change years ago, embarrassingly enough, some you may still struggle with.

You may struggle with exercise, getting to the gym, or doing any exercise at all.

You may struggle with patience, we want it now! Instant gratification, in this microwave society that we live in.

Funnily enough, I struggle with procrastination.

I struggle with budgeting my finances, I like clothes and shoes! Did I say like? I LOVE clothes and shoes.

I struggle with spending enough time studying.

I struggle with spending enough quality time with others who need my help.

I struggle with paying attention and I am easily distracted, looking at and thinking about the things I shouldn't. I had to learn and discipline myself.

At times I struggle with anxiety.

All of these enemies have been with me for a long time. My school report card at the age of five, six, and seven would say "a bright and gifted child, but easily distracted.

You see, my predictable enemy has been around for quite a while!

If you are really honest with yourself, you would admit to having them too.

Enemies that have predictable patterns.

If you can figure out and master the game, you win the game.

Go ahead, put in the work and figure out the pattern of your enemy, break the pattern, and then WIN!

Your Thoughts..........

What Do You Do When Your Past HOLDS You Hostage?

Well what do you do??? Isn't that the million dollar/pound/euro/ yen question? First things first, let's not confuse insecurity with fear, although they are very similar in meaning as the definitions below show;

FEAR – a distressing emotion aroused by impending danger, evil, pain, etc., whether the threat is real or imagined; the feeling or condition of being afraid. Synonyms: foreboding, apprehension, consternation, dismay, dread, terror, fright, panic, horror, trepidation, qualm. Antonyms: courage, security, calm, intrepidity.

INSECRE – subject to fears, doubts, etc.; not self-confident or assured: an insecure person.

"The fears we do not face, become the walls that imprison us"

I remember a few years ago (OK, so it was 21 years ago to be exact), being in a job where I was constantly berated and belittled. I was a Marketing Assistant and worked for two guys that although were quite generous with gifts when they travelled, were always angry and hostile in the office. I remember the look of pity the other girls would give, and the other Marketing Managers (who were all women) would all console me. At the time, it felt as though nothing I did was good enough and the "there, there, never mind, poor thing" from my colleagues added to the humiliation. The PA to the MD spoke up for me and told him, he called me into his office and asked me what had been going on, I told him everything, warts and all. He sent me home and told me he would look into it. When he called to tell me that there was no need for me to return to work, well that told me what I was worth to them, a big fat NOTHING.

And so, the pattern continued for many, many years, in many different jobs, And, yes, I believed it when they told me I deserved to be spoken to like that.

Now, here's the thing, at no point did they ever in so many words tell me I deserved to be spoken to like I was beneath them. But the fear of losing my job and not being able to pay my bills made me "allow" them to speak to me like that. So, in fact, I was telling them that, that is how I deserved to be treated and spoken to.

My way of dealing with it was to not tell a soul, (look what happened the last time a person spoke up for me, I was let go).

So, I would look for another job, get the job and then be sworn at, shouted at, and belittled all over again. I started to believe the problem was with me and that I just couldn't do the job right. So, every job that I got, I would go to work with FEAR. And because of that fear, I would be nervous and anxious while at work, and would spend any holiday time worried that my work never measured up and that I just wasn't competent.

One of the worse instances was I had an employer who would like to openly swear and shout at me in front of everyone in the office, and I would stay silent. One day, my boss decided that I had to update him every day on what I was working on. During this time, one particular day, he took me out for coffee (I HATE COFFEE) and calmly said to me "I know you've had bereavements and I know your mother is sick, but it's not my f- -king problem, is it?", Oh yeah, did I forget to mention that my mother had just an operation on both her feet and three days later my uncle died suddenly while he was at home, so it had been a bit of an emotional four days before this conversation.

F – False

E – Evidence

A – Appearing

R - Real

Yet again, I said nothing as he continued to tell me that he feels as though I am not on top of things (even though in my performance review, he told me I was an asset to the company). Then he went on to tell me he would like for me to take on more responsibility by taking on the project of overseeing the build-out and opening of a new branch.

Needless to say, I put my resume up on several job boards the very same day!!! When I handed in my resignation, he got so mad and asked me what had brought this on and asked me to stay, several times! That was a no for me.

But then it hit me, I wasn't incompetent, I didn't deserve to be spoken to like that, I was afraid. I was afraid that if I spoke up, I would be seen as an aggressive woman, because you know we are not assertive when we speak up for ourselves, we're aggressive and it would go against me when it was time for promotions, etc. I believed the treatment I had received in the past and let it dictate how I would be treated in the future. I let this happen to me because I was afraid. I let my past experiences hold me hostage to accept any treatment that was dished out to me.

The weird thing about this is that in all other areas of my life no one would DARE even let the thought cross their minds to speak to me like this. I was known to jump in a person's throat faster than they could blink if they even attempted to disrespect me in such a way.

So what was the difference? By nature, I am not an insecure person, but I have to admit to being gripped by fear. I needed to work on me and how I could turn this around since I couldn't continue going through my working life like this, a new job almost every year. I needed fixing and it had to start with ME. I had to believe that I could do the job I was employed to do, and I could do it well, I had the God-given ability and talent.

I got another job, all was going well, I had three bosses, one was the nicest, nurturing, and patient boss you could have. He would take time to explain things he was working on even if it wasn't directly relevant to what I was working on. He would answer questions and genuinely cared about his staff and their wellbeing. One I barely saw, and the other, well, all I can say is he was the type of person that wouldn't tell you directly if you made a mistake. He would wait until we were in meetings to mention it. For instance, I circulated an agenda for a management meeting two days prior to the meeting. I had misspelt a person's name and rather than tell me, he came into the meeting pronouncing the person's name the way it was misspelt, thereby alerting everyone else in the meeting about the error.

He would nitpick and criticize any work that I sent him. Even though he was not the only person to get the work, he would be the only person to literally tear it apart. In my mind, it was here we go again, I felt like Sisyphus from Greek mythology, eternally pushing a boulder up a hill only for it to come rolling back down once he neared the top.

He was so bad that other colleagues had to report him to HR. He went as far as bringing a disciplinary hearing against another person, but it all got thrown out. He was that bad. The relief in my mind was "at least, it's not just me." But the truth was that regardless of whether it was a case of him just being a mean-spirited person, I still had to confront what it did to me, I couldn't hide behind "oh well, that is just how he is".

I learnt the adage—"there is more than one way to skin a cat"—to be true, I approached my boss in a very calm manner and I apologized to him. Wait now, before you start shouting and rolling your eyes at the page. I started by apologizing to him, as I wanted to let him know that the way I had responded to his behavior wasn't right. I should not have let it affect me in the way I had. It affected the communication, making our work harder than it needed to be. The truth was I used to call the walk to his office the green mile. He then in turn apologized to me and explained why he behaved the way he did towards me and we were able to discuss a better way of working together moving forward.

I was not seen as the aggressive, angry woman, but a peacemaker that was able to calmly and rationally discuss a problem and work on a forward-thinking resolution. The truth is, and believe me, I really wanted to tell him about himself in the worst possible way, leaving nothing out, but that really would have been the end of that job and fed a stereotype. And why give the smug so and so the satisfaction.

I was so nervous about having the conversation with him that I agonized over what I was going to say, if it would jeopardize my job or, make me look confrontational. A million things went through my mind and I had that horrible gut-churning, nail-biting (and I don't bite my nails), can't-focus feeling. But I knew that to exorcise the spirit of fear that gripped me, I needed to make the first step. And that first step was to have an open discussion with the person I believed was instilling the fear within me. It was the first step on the road to getting past that particular fear. And I didn't know it at the time, but I took his power away.

Now don't get me wrong, I am not all the way there yet. There are times that I still feel anxiety about work, especially if I have made a mistake or forgotten to do something. There are still times that I wake up fearful, but I have to remind myself that no one is perfect, and we all make mistakes. Remember, it's not always the mistake you make but how you work to get past it, how you fix it, and most importantly, what you learn from it that matters. No one has the right to make you feel like you are not good enough.

A popular saying goes "I'm not where I want to be, but thank God I'm not where I used to be." But I know that with God's help and a LOT of prayer, I will get there.

I have learnt through all of this to NEVER allow anyone to disrespect me in such a way, regardless of who they are.

I have learnt that I deserve to be spoken to and treated with respect.

I have learnt that people will only do what I allow them to get away with.

So, what are you allowing fear to do to you?

"The conductor has to turn their back to the crowd to lead the orchestra. That is how beautiful melodies are made."

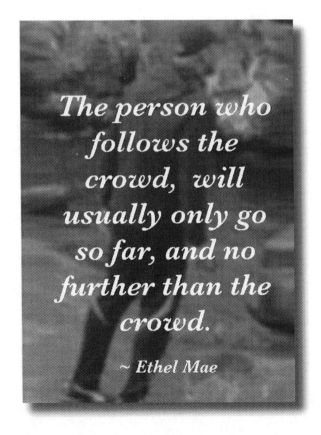

The person who follows the crowd, will usually only go so far, and no further than the crowd.

~ Ethel Mae

Your Thoughts..........

_____

_____

_____

_____

_____

_____

_____

_____

_____

_____

_____

_____

_____

"How can you embrace the future when you are still holding on to the past? You can't hold anything new with closed hands full of stuff."

So, Who Wins?

There is a battle of two
wolves Inside us all
One is evil, it is
anger, Jealousy greed,
resentment, Lies,
inferiority and ego.
The other is good, it is
joy, peace Love, hope, humility, kindness Empathy and truth.
The wolf that wins? The one you feed.
~ Cherokee Proverb

This Cherokee Proverb speaks volumes doesn't it? But it is a question we all need to ask ourselves. What am I allowing to consume me? What are my predominant thoughts? What am I focusing on? All very simple basic questions, but all very important questions we need to ask ourselves.

Let's look into this a bit further. Something has happened to you or someone has done something to hurt or upset you. What are your thoughts immediately after or whenever you think of that situation or that person? If you can answer this with "I hold nothing against them and wish them well" that is great. Do that, we need more of that, keep feeding that wolf. But if your thoughts are thoughts of anger, resentment, thoughts of revenge and unforgiveness, well you are feeding the wrong wolf.

We've all been there, we have all been on the receiving end of hurtful behavior, or circumstances where we have been adversely affected. I will even go as far as saying that some of us have been the person inflicting the pain, whether intentionally or unintentionally.

So what do we do? I'm not saying the you should act like nothing has happened, or deny the painful feelings. That's far from it since denial is good for no one and doesn't help you to heal. What I am saying is, that for your own peace and sanity, you will need to release the person and/or circumstance and forgive them.

I remember going through a breakup where the person had lied to me about important things, namely a "friend" he had. When I found out the truth, I was so hurt, upset, and I felt a total sense of betrayal. I ended the relationship, cut him off and made sure he knew that I knew what he had done and that I had found out the truth. In the days, weeks, and months that followed, I was angry, and whenever he called me, I had such a stand offish attitude towards him, I was abrupt and I let him know at every chance I got that it was "his fault that I was hurt" and guilted him with it."

Now I thought I had every right to, right? After all, HE was the one who lied, HE was the one that used and abused my trust, He was the one who caused the upset and pain. I felt completely justified in my behavior! It never occurred to me that I was holding on to pain, I was entertaining anger and resentment. I would have full blown arguments with him... in my head. And during those arguments, I really gave him what for! He didn't just get a piece of my mind, he got the whole lot. I told him alright!

It wasn't until a day that I was thinking about him (again!). Having yet another in my head argument that I realized that I was sitting down wound so tight, my breathing was shallow and erratic, and I was so tense. That is when I decided that I couldn't carry on that way. I then thought a bit deeper about other behaviors within myself, having trouble sleeping, concentrating, and it even affected my appetite.

Right then I made the decision not to continue giving him that much power over me. I decided that I was better than that and even more importantly, he really didn't deserve that much of my time or energy.

To stay in line with the wolf theme, I went away to lick my wounds. I took the time to be kind to myself and accept that yes I had been treated unfairly, yes, I had been lied to but no, I didn't have the right to hold on to it, I had to let it go. Really, for all the time I thought I was hurting him back and spiteing him, I was actually hurting myself, was he tense and stressed? Was he not sleeping properly? Was his appetite affected? I don't know, and quite frankly, it is not my concern. I am my concern!

I once read that by holding on to these negative feelings and unforgiveness, you are drinking poison and waiting for it to affect the other person. Think on that for a moment, you are doing damage to your mental and, in some cases, physical state and expecting the other person to suffer as a result. Doesn't make sense does it?

When you find these times that your mind drifts to the person or situation. The moment you catch yourself in that space, IMMEDIATELY change what you are thinking about. Don't continue in that frame of mind, no matter how much you want to be in that moment and finish your imaginary confrontation and make your point! Put on some music if you are in a place where you can do so, go for a walk, talk to someone (about something unrelated to your thoughts). Just do whatever you need to do to STOP FEEDING THAT WOLF! You deserve it, you are worth it

I am not here to tell you it wil happen suddenly. I am not going to tell you that all you need to do is think positively. That is only a part of it.

It will take time and practice and it will take you being patient with yourself. You will thank you for it and before you know it, you'll begin to feel nothing but peace and calm whenever you think of that person or situation. It won't happen overnight, but I promise you it will happen and it will be worth it.

So, who wins? That is up to you. FEED THE RIGHT WOLF!

Your Thoughts..........

_____

_____

_____

_____

_____

_____

_____

_____

_____

_____

_____

_____

_____

_____

Choose to Forgive

Choosing to Forgive . . .

Unlocks the Cell to the Prison inside your heart - it sets YOU free!

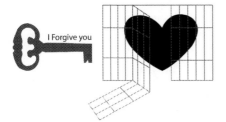

I Forgive you

What if I told you that holding on to unforgiveness only affects you? What if I also told you that holding on to unforgiveness hurts you more than anything or anyone else. You see, unforgiveness is nothing other than holding on to hurt, pain, and thoughts of revenge.

The dictionary definition of forgiveness is 'to stop feeling anger toward (someone who has done something wrong): to stop blaming (someone)' or 'to give up resentment of or claim to requital for *<forgive an insult>*'

Therefore, unforgiveness is the opposite, it is feeling anger, projecting blame, and holding on to resentment. Which ultimately only hurts you. Surely, I can't be the only person that has been angry with someone who has hurt me. I mean really angry to the point where I have visualized all kinds of revenge on them.

I have played and replayed arguments with them in my mind where I have gotten everything off my chest. Only to see them or hear about how GREAT they are doing and how wonderful their life is and how they have moved on!!! That, in itself, would get me even angrier, as I would then think "don't you remember or think about what you did to me?" "I want you to feel what I am feeling, I want you to feel and acknowledge what you put me through." But they were happy living their life without even a backward glance in my direction.

So, what does that tell you? Unforgiveness only affects YOU, unforgiveness only hurts YOU, no one else but YOU!!!! And that in turn manifests itself as bitterness, anger, and drives people away, which then leads to loneliness.

But it doesn't have to be that way, it really doesn't. You can choose to forgive, you can choose to let go of the hurt, pain, and anger.

Forgiveness takes strength, mustering up genuine compassion for those who have wronged you, instead of allowing anger towards them to eat away at you. Letting it go or burying the hatchet brings peace to your heart, mind, and soul. The peace you will feel is unbelievable, it will make you wonder why you hadn't forgiven sooner.

Now you do have some people who are naturally forgiving. They have this amazing ability to not only forgive others but also to forgive themselves. But for those of us—yes, I said us—who this doesn't come that easily or naturally to, we have to do some work and digging deep to find the strength to forgive. We have to get past what was done, stop focusing on who did what, and look within for inner strength to forgive.

Studies have found that people who are able to forgive actually live longer. There is a book by Dr. Dick Tibbits titled *Forgive to Live*. So, you see, talking about forgiveness isn't cliché, it is a life saver. Studies have gone as far as investigating the relationship between forgiveness, spirituality, health, and mortality, in a national U.S. sample of 1500 adults aged 66 and older. The study published in the Journal of Behavioral Medicine was the first to show long life as one of the benefits of forgiveness.

When you make the decision to forgive, you choose to give up feelings of resentment and the need for revenge. This will also help you to stop being judgmental of yourself and the person/people who hurt you. The need for revenge, feelings of resentment, and judgment are then replaced by compassion, kindness, and love.

> *"Forgiveness does not change the past,*
> *but it does change the future."*

Now, in all this, I am not telling you to behave as though you haven't had an experience that has caused you great pain. You will in evidently remember from time to time what was done to you. And forgiveness does not make excuses for the hurt caused to you. But rather than dwell and wallow in thoughts and feelings that are negative and harmful to you, reverse the negative feelings with positive actions, positive thoughts and positive feelings.

When you forgive, it has to be without conditions. When you attached conditions such as "I will forgive them if they apologize" or remind the person of what they did when you see them or have a disagreement until they promise never to do it again. This is a sure indication that there is still resentment lurking under the surface, and you haven't truly forgiven.

Just imagine that the person who hurt you died or moved to another country, and you can't get the apology or closure that you hoped for or believed you deserved; Will you hold and carry that pain forever? Closure with the person or situation that caused pain may never come and you have to be alright with that.

Continuing to harbor resentment, hurts you mentally and physically. It keeps your stress levels high and I am sure we have all heard the expression 'stress kills.' True forgiveness comes from a conscious decision to let go of the hurt and pain. You have to be OK with the apology you never got and still be able to forgive! Studies have also shown that those who choose to forgive are less prone to being anxious or depressed. These attributes could all contribute to living a longer more fulfilling life.

Forgiveness
The Key to Freedom

So, to round things off, if you want to be a truly forgiving person, you have to start with you, by making the decision to forgive, whether those who have wronged you apologize or not. Because really, it is not about them, it is about you! It is about your mental health, your physical health, your spiritual health and ultimately, it will prolong your life. Start today, make up your mind today to forgive, make up your mind to let it go, make up your mind to live longer. Start now, start today, and do it for you!

What are you waiting for? Choose to Forgive, you can do it, it's not easy but it's oh so worth it!

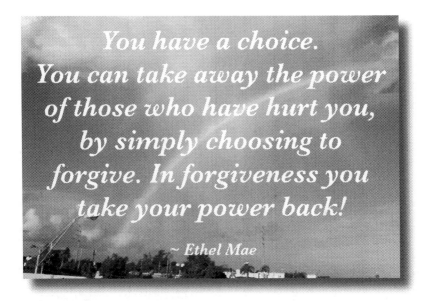

You have a choice. You can take away the power of those who have hurt you, by simply choosing to forgive. In forgiveness you take your power back!

~ Ethel Mae

Your Thoughts..........

_____

_____

_____

_____

_____

_____

_____

_____

_____

_____

_____

_____

_____

What's Inside of You?

We've all said it, "ever since they were promoted they've changed", or "ever since they got a bit of power they've changed", or "since they got more/came into money", or "since they got married" etc. the list could go on.

If I were to squeeze an orange as hard as I could, what would come out? Orange juice, of course. Not apple juice, not grapefruit juice, not lemon juice, but orange juice.

Why? This may seem like a silly question but bear with me. Why, when you squeeze an orange does orange juice come out? Well, it's an orange and that's what's inside.

Put yourself in the place of the orange, and someone "squeezes" you, puts pressure on you, says something you don't like, offends you or upsets you. And out of you comes anger, hatred, bitterness, fear. Why? Because that's what's inside. If understanding, forgiveness, compassion and peace is what you show. Why? Because that is what is inside of you.

It's one of the great lessons of life. To stop and take an inward look at what comes out when life "squeezes" you, puts pressure on you. When someone upsets, hurts or offends you or you "change". If it is negative reactions and emotions that come out of you, it's because that's what's inside. It doesn't matter who or what does the "squeezing", your partner, your parents, your siblings, your children, your boss, the government, it could even be a complete stranger. Ultimately, what spills out of you is what's inside. And what's inside is up to you, it's your choice.

It is very easy to fake it and put on a front, that is until you are "squeezed". There are many parading around with the façade of being peace and love and love and light.

We have all seen it, someone that we thought were more Zen than the Dalai Lama completely lose it when a simple issue arises, they get a promotion, or money and they "change" etc. Then we have also seen the person with the temperament of the Tasmanian Devil react completely calmly in a situation that we thought they would have flipped

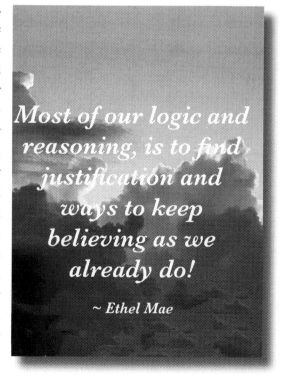

Most of our logic and reasoning, is to find justification and ways to keep believing as we already do!

~ Ethel Mae

out in. All it takes is the right circumstance, the right "squeeze" to reveal the inner truth of who you are. When someone puts the pressure on you, squeezes you and out of you comes anything other than peace, it's because that's what you've allowed to be inside and take root. Once you take away all the negative responses you don't want in your life and replace them with inner peace and love, you'll find yourself living a highly optimal functioning life.

A life where you are less tense. A life where you feel less physical pain. The mind and body are one. You would be surprised at how much of the pain you feel in your body is a manifestation of your thoughts and your heart content. High blood pressure, diabetes, headaches, back pain and there is more. Often can be traced back to holding on to resentments and unforgiveness. There was even an article written of this by John Hopkins Medicine, entitled *Forgiveness: Your Health Depends on It.*

To do this, a little (or a lot) of inner reflection and searching is needed. Why are you angry? It may not be apparent to others but deep down, if you are easily irritated take a look at why and what are your triggers, get to the root of what it is and make the decision to tackle it and change. Make the decision to not allow external factors to affect your inner peace or your physical being.

So, the next time you think someone has "changed" or been "squeezed" and react either positively or negatively. Have they really changed or reacted out of character, or could it just be that their real inner self has been revealed?

So, what is on the inside of you?

"There is a story they tell of two dogs. Both at separate times walk into the same room. One comes out wagging his tail while the other comes out growling. A woman watching this goes into the room to see what could possibly make one dog so happy and the other so sad. To her surprise, she found a room filled with mirrors. The happy dog found a thousand happy dogs looking back at him while the angry dog saw only angry dogs growling back to him. What you see in the world around you is a reflection of who you are"
~ Unknown

Your Thoughts..........

"There is something very therapeutic
about looking up at the sky.
The sun setting and the moon rising.
The clouds moving silently across the sky.
Just taking a deep breath and reflecting.
Watching day turn to night
and night turn to day.
Contemplating the effortlessness
of the changing of time."

Just as a diamond is made from a piece of coal after it has gone through immense pressure. And pure gold is made after being purified through intense heat and fire. So too shall you arise and be blessed. Precious stones and precious metals go through pressure and heat to become valuable and priceless commodities.

Just as life will take you through fire and pressure. This is just a process, just a season, and this too shall pass. Keep going through.

Gold must go through fire to be melted in order to be purified

There are times that I look over my life and where I am now and I can't help but smile. I am able to took back over my life, the road I have travelled and can appreciate my now. Knowing that my now could have been very different. I look at the hardships and know that I didn't have to get back up. The times I had doubts and fears and know that I didn't have to have faith and believe again. I looked at the now healed me and remember the hurt. If I could meet you to show you that, trust me my brother, trust me my sister, this too, shall pass! But as gold and diamonds must go through heat and pressure for their value to be seen and known. Your value, your strength to will come through.

Diamonds start out as coal

But He knows the way that I take; when He has tried/ tested me, I shall come forth as gold.
~Job 21:10

Your Thoughts..........

Pay Attention to Who Claps When You Win

You know who your friends are, right? At least, you hope you do! We all believe we know who our 'ride or dies' are, the ones who have our backs through thick and thin.

But life has a funny way of showing you who your true friends and supporters are, who is real. Sometimes, you learn the hard way and other times, they reveal themselves. I recently read a quote, "Be careful who you let on your boat, not everyone is rowing with you, some are actually drilling holes."

It is a very painful feeling when your closest friend or friends pull away from you, when your life begins to change for the better, you get married, or you begin to achieve a level of success. The people that you thought would be happy for you and always there for you, eventually you come to the cold harsh reality that they only wanted you to do well, just as long as you are not doing better than them. These people were never really your friend.

If you take a step back and look. Were there any red flags? Was there ever a time that something was said to you or about you, that was a bit of a put down but passed off as "you know I didn't mean anything by it, I was only joking?" Pay attention to that!

Your friend, your real friend wouldn't do that. A true friend would not say anything derogatory about you or let anyone else for that matter.

Were there times when you felt as though they didn't support you as you did them? A true friend would be there for you as much as you are for them. Any true relationship cannot survive without reciprocity. You need to ask yourself are you getting more than you're giving?

Unfortunately, many times the true intentions and the hearts of these "friends" and their loyalty is revealed after you have built up a relationship with them, trusted them and given your friendship and loyalty to them.

Be proud of yourself for being a good friend to them. Sometimes the reason for staying hurt, is because of a belief that everyone you have a connection, a friendship with is going to be in your life for all of your life. This is just not so, as the poem says, *people come into your life for a reason, a season or a lifetime.* The hurt comes when trying to may seasonal friend's lifetime friends. Wish them well and let them go.

At times in life, you are thrown under the bus more often than being helped onto the bus. But you still keep going. Giving up or giving in is never an option.

Sometimes, you will just have to clap for yourself, pat your own back, encourage yourself and cheer you on!

"Live each day in expectation that all you are believing for will happen.

The right doors at the right time will all be opened for you, just be ready to walk through.

Be excited, prepare yourself to receive all you are hoping and praying for and keep on walking ahead.

Get ready, doors are always opening for you."

"Finally living my life as I've imagined, blessed, and favored.

So grateful and appreciative for all I am and all I have.

Note to you:
Today you are the most exquisite, stunning and intelligent that you have ever been, until tomorrow. Tomorrow you will be even more exquisite, stunning and intelligent.

~ Ethel Mae

For blessings past and blessings yet to come.

For those who have come and those who have gone and those that remain."

Your Thoughts..........

"I no longer have patience for certain things, not because I've become arrogant, but simply because I reached a point in my life where I do not want to waste more time with what displeases me or hurts me. I have no patience for cynicism, excessive criticism, and demands of any nature. I lost the will to please those who do not like me, I have to love those who do not love me and smile at those who do not want to smile at me. I must be the light.

I no longer spend a single minute on those who lie or want to manipulate, but I do pray for them. I decided not to coexist anymore with pretense, hypocrisy, dishonesty and cheap praise. I do not tolerate selective erudition nor academic arrogance. I do not adjust either to popular gossiping. I hate conflict and comparisons. In friendship, I dislike the lack of loyalty and betrayal. I do not get along with those who do not know how to give a compliment or a word of encouragement. Exaggerations bore me and I try to avoid those with rigid or inflexible personalities. And on top of everything, I have no patience for anyone who does not deserve my patience, although I am trying since I am far from perfect. I need God's grace more than ever before."

~ As said by Meryl Streep and edited and adapted to me.

Thank you for showing me such love. I am very humbled and blessed. For too long, I've not been happy with how I look. And realized this came from being told 'you're so skinny, do you even eat?' Or 'you're too dark', 'your teeth are crooked.' But I have learnt to love my skinny, dark skin, and crooked-teeth self. NEVER EVER allow the negative comments or opinions of others make you feel any less than your fabulous, beautiful,

That man, that woman, That man, that woman may not have had the best start in life. Their current situation may be far from ideal, but one thing they will never do is give up. Their heart is beautiful yet tough from lifes fight as they take care of themselves, their family and take care business. They know the cards they have been dealt will change into a winning hand, why? Because giving up is never an option.

~ Ethel Mae

and best self. It doesn't matter what you look like, tall or short, dark or fair, or whether you have straight teeth, crooked teeth, white teeth, yellow teeth, or no teeth. It doesn't matter what you sound like, you are beautiful, you are God's masterpiece. Love how God made you and no one will be able to shake that. Silence the critics!

I love you, you beautiful, blessed, marvelous person, have an AMAZING day!

God has blessed and favored me more than I could ever have asked or imagined. I am beyond, honored, content, and forever grateful; my heart is so full. Feeling great and good about myself. "I am fearfully and wonderfully made." This is what favor looks like.

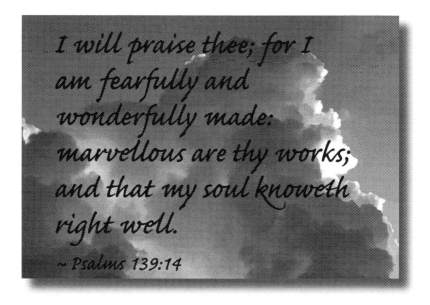

I will praise thee; for I am fearfully and wonderfully made: marvellous are thy works; and that my soul knoweth right well.
~ Psalms 139:14

No more allowing anyone to make me feel bad or ashamed of who I am and whose I am.

"Just because you can relate to and identify with the negative behavior, doesn't mean you have to adopt the mindset."

Be bold... The opposite of fear is boldness.

"Be not afraid" and "fear not" are mentioned in the bible over 100 times. Get the message?

> *Fear not, for I am with you;*
> *Be not dismayed, for*
> *I am your God.*
> *I will strengthen you,*
> *Yes, I will help you,*
> *I will uphold you with My*
> *righteous right hand.'*
>
> *~ Isaiah 41:10*

Because, no one can block the blessings that God has for you. What's for you is for YOU!

Your Thoughts.........

"Being extremely grateful and appreciative for all I have, all I am, and the people who have helped me along the way.

I pray I never get too wrapped up in myself, my own agenda and my success to forget those who have helped me, supported me, and truly love me."

Use things and love people, don't use people and love things.

As Oscar Wilde put it, "Nowadays people know the price of everything and the value of nothing."

"Keep pursuing excellence in all you do. The road will be hard at times, but don't give up.

Even when people no longer believe in you, don't quit, stand firm, keep pushing, you will and can do it.

Hard work and self-belief pays off!"

You have the courage to overcome difficult situations. You have the courage to go after all of your goals. You defend what you believe in and won't compromise your values or virtue, because you are a person of substance.

~ Ethel Mae

Your Thoughts..........

"I thank You! I thank You! I thank You! For You are an awesome God! Lord of the world, Master of the Universe. I humbly and boldly stand before You this day giving You honor, glory and praise for all that You are, and for all that You have allowed me to be. Only by faith have I made it this far. You have given me the gift of forgiveness, and the ability to see myself as forgiven from all the things that have kept me from believing that I was worthy of Your love and blessings. I am faith-full and free from all judgment, fear, doubt, and shame. I see anew when I look in the mirror, my spirit is free. I rejoice, and I give You all the praise! God, I thank! I thank You! I thank You! Amen."

Weeping is Only for a Night, Your Joy is Coming

Weeping may endure for a night, But joy comes in the morning.

Psalms 30:5

No matter how long the night feels morning HAS TO FOLLOW. How often have you gone to bed and woken up to feel as though you only slept for a few minutes? And other times you have gone to bed at the same time and felt as though you have had a nice long sleep. My point is no matter how long or short the night feels and seems, morning HAS TO FOLLOW.

No matter what it is you are going through, it will pass. It may seem as though it is lasting forever, but it won't! You will get through this. Just hold on a little while longer, things will get better, things will work out for your good, but you MUST BELIEVE it will. You must have hope and have faith that things will turn around. Your joy is on the way.

Are You Ready for Your Fairytale?

I have read numerous posts that say, "a real man would do this," or "a real man would do that," or "a real man would have his stuff together." I have also read, "The man God has for you will be this," and "the Man God has for you will be that," and "he will have all his stuff together, be your peace," blah, blah, blah!

But just supposing the man God has for you is a man that has been through a horrible divorce, who has been mentally broken, and had his heart ripped out of his chest. Because, let's face it, some women are broken and, in turn, hurt the "good/real" men because of their brokenness. Yes, the same goes for some broken men who hurt, use and devastate women.

I have heard many horror stories where men, good men, have been treated so badly by their mothers, ex-wives, wives, ex-girlfriends, girlfriends, the mother of their child or children or by women in general that it has left them so disillusioned with love and relationships. They are afraid to put their hearts back out there. But it doesn't make them any less a "real man" or a "man of God." In my opinion, it makes them more of a real man as they have experienced life!

We have the erroneous thinking that it is only women that get the short straw when it comes to heartache, because all men are dogs right? WRONG! We couldn't be more wrong. Our men are hurting and dying because we have romanticized what a real man is, thanks to social media and #relationshipgoals. But a real man is the man that has been hurt, had his heart broken, taken a beating from life, and still gets up each day to try to face life. Albeit, emotionally shut down.

The older we get, the higher the likelihood that life will happen to us and we will be hurt, we will experience heartache, betrayal, and possibly humiliation. Which can defeat even the best of us. What if the man God has for you is your assignment to Love the hurt away and to love him back to emotional health? In some cases, it could literally be love him back to life.

With all the "real man/man God has for you" talk floating around, so many are missing out on seeing good, real, honest, hardworking men because they are looking through rose-colored glasses for the fairytale.

They are expecting prince charming to come swooping in on his white horse, buff to the max (now, I'm not saying anything is wrong with a buff man, that's how I like 'em ;o)), financially secure, with a good job and a heart of gold. Supposing he had all of that and life, divorce, bad investments, the economy or incarceration happened and left him depleted? And now, he looks more like a man with scars and war wounds. Would you still overlook him? Because if he loved once, chances are he is able to love again. If he was financially secure, etc. chances are he can get back on his feet again and be even more successful having learnt valuable life lessons. This time, with the right woman by his side. My view, if you can't ride with me when I am down, please don't expect to get in the car to ride with me when I am back up.

Look at the fairytales, there is not one that had ended in "true love" that didn't go through difficulties and struggles to get there.

Beauty and the Beast, the beast had to live under a curse that turned him from a handsome gentleman into a beast. Only true love was able to undo the years of pain and torment of having to live as a beast, because the beast is not who he truly was. But in order for Beauty to love him, she had to get to know him and see past the beast. He had to get past his own insecurities that everyone was judging him by based on his current circumstances. After he went through all of that, a woman's love is what helped to emotionally heal him and love him back to life and health!

Sleeping Beauty, a curse was spoken over her life as a baby. She was stripped of her identity, hidden away for the first sixteen years of her life not knowing she was a Princess. Went through a rebellious stage of running away when she found out who she really was, trying to discover herself, find her identity. She fell into a trance that led her into danger. Then had to experience the pain of pricking her finger and falling into a coma. After she went through *all* of that, *then*, Prince Charming came along, and love saved her! Yes, he saved her, but it could well be the other way around.

Snow White, she had an evil stepmother that was jealous of her. She had to run away for her own safety, she then moved in and lived with S E V E N crazy men with different personalities (all those different personality traits could be in one man). Her Stepmother

eventually found out she was still alive, hunted her down, disguised herself, poisoned her, she then fell into a coma. After she went through all of that, Prince Charming came along, and love saved her! Yes, he saved her, but again, it could well be the other way around.

Cinderella, her father died. She was left with a stepmother and stepsisters who treated her like a slave for years. In order to break free she had to disguise herself and pretend to be someone else. She was hidden away when the prince came and denied the opportunity to try the shoe on. She had to push through to be seen and given the chance to try the shoe. After she went through all of that, Prince Charming came along and saved her! Yes, he saved her, but again, it could well be the other way around.

Princess Fiona in Shrek, she was only able to be her true self at night behind closed doors. But the "real man" loved her in her ogre state. Not as the beautifully made up princess, but for who she truly was. She was loved for her, not for the false perception, not for who people thought she should be. She was at her happiest when she was an Ogre and miserable when she had to fake it as the Princess.

The Frog, it wasn't until a woman looked past the frog state and kissed him that he became a Prince.

You see where I am going with this?

Men and women, come with a past and many times, it is how they are treated after they have been hurt, divorced, etc. that could set the trajectory for how they love for the rest of their lives. My point, "real men" or "the man God has for you" may well come with scars, some of them come maimed and limping. Don't overlook a "real man" because of a smoke screen put up by social media, that "a real man" is perfect. He may not have a white horse, he may have a bike, he may be riding the bus or he may even be walking. He may not own a house, as he left it in the divorce or he left the children with their mother in the house. He may not have a fat bank account as the lawyers in the divorce or bad investments swallowed it all.

But as in the fairytales to have the happily ever after, they all went through some serious challenges to get there. They all had to go through stuff! What would have happened if the prince looked at Sleeping Beauty, Snow White and said, "well, she can't be a REAL woman, or the woman God has for me because she's got issues." Or if the Prince looked at Cinderella and said, "her family is crazy, ain't nobody got time for all that!"

Don't misunderstand me, there are some men that lack ambition, some that are happy to live off other people and not work, and some that are just straight rotten, dishonest, users, abusers, and cheaters. There are also women out there like that! These are not who I am referring to (they are for another article!).

If we must use social media for #relationshipgoals, let's look at the status updates where men post how proud they are of the woman that was with them through thick and thin. Or the woman that loved them when they were on their face and had nothing. I love when I see status updates that say, "she was with me when I had nothing, so now I have it I will give her everything."

And yes, I know there are men that will trade the 'ride or die' in the minute they have made it, for the younger, hotter version. Yes, I have seen waiting to exhale! Again, this isn't about those ones.

EVERY STRONG MAN NEEDS A STRONG WOMAN TO LIFT HIM UP WHEN HE'S DOWN

What happens when the good man, the real man, the man God has for you needs to be loved back to health and life? When the love and care of a good woman is exactly what they need. Let's face it, there has been a time when we were all broken and hurt, for one reason or another. And hoped at those times to be shown love, understanding and compassion.

I love the song by Eric Benet "Love the Hurt Away." It is about a woman that has been hurt and lied to in her relationship and his love will help her to heal and to love again, if she will give him the chance.

You can still have #relationshipgoals but you must be real and accept that your Prince Charming, your King, may come to you scarred, scared, hurt, and limping. Because at some point, we all have been there.

So, are you sure you are ready for your fairytale?

Love the Hurt Away – Eric Benet

They broke your heart and took your pride
Will you ever love again?
Though you try you don't believe it
Come over here, talk to me a while
If you tried you would find that,
Someone like me, simple and free
I could change your mind,
Love the hurt away, that's all I want to do.

Your Thoughts..........

"Don't get set into one form, adapt it and let it grow, be like water.

Empty your mind, be formless, shapeless — like water.

Now you put water in a cup, it becomes the cup; You put water into a bottle, it becomes the bottle; You put it in a teapot, it becomes the teapot.

Now water can flow or it can crash. Be water, my friend."

Good Thoughts
Bad Thoughts

An excerpt by George Clinton leader of the music group Parliament Funkadelic from the CD *Standing On The Verge Of Getting It On*.

Change your mind, and you change your relation to time.

Your life is the reproduction of your thoughts.

Free your mind and your ass will follow. Be careful of the thought-seeds you plant in the garden of your mind.

For seeds grow after their kind.

Every thought takes roots in your subconscious.

Blossoms sooner or later into an act, And bears its own fruit.

Good thoughts bring forth good fruit.

Your Thoughts.........

_____

_____

_____

_____

_____

_____

_____

_____

_____

_____

_____

_____

_____

_____

"Forgiveness is having the courage to take down the walls that we think are there to protect us."

Your Thoughts..........

_____

_____

_____

_____

_____

_____

_____

_____

_____

_____

_____

_____

_____

_____

It's All in Your Mind

Whatever you hold in your mind will have a way of occurring in your life.

If you continue to think and believe as you always have and act as you always have, you will keep getting what you have always gotten.

You can't keep walking around the same mountain and expect a different view. In order to have a different experience, you have to change what you are doing

We need to learn how to manage and select our thoughts, the same way we think about and select what to wear each day.
If we want to truly take control of our life, we must work on our mind, our thoughts.
Our thoughts, not people is the only thing we should ever be trying to control!

~ Ethel Mae

If you want different results in your life, they key is to change your mind.

"Forgeries of happiness. The stuff we buy/acquire under the illusion that, that is what will make us happy. When really that is just an empty substitute"

"Faith is exactly what it takes to get through uncertainty. Faith is not necessary when you know how things are going to work out - that's knowledge. It's in the time of unknowing that having faith is what sees you through to the other side. Faith is what gives you strength. Faith is that light in your heart that keeps on shining even when it's all darkness outside. Now is the time to keep that faith alive. Believe and have faith!"

Your Thoughts..........

The Beatitudes

In life, you will experience hurt at the hands of others, sometimes, they may not intend it and sometimes, they may well do. Regardless of this, life still goes on and you have to learn how to forgive, let it go, and not become angry or bitter. Many times in life, you try to do good, only for it to be taken the wrong way, but regardless, you must still continue to do what is right and carry on even though you may be hurting.

3, Blessed are the poor in spirit, for theirs is the kingdom of heaven.

4, Blessed are those who mourn, for they will be comforted.

5, Blessed are the meek, for they will inherit the earth.

6, Blessed are those who hunger and thirst after righteousness, for they will be filled.

7, Blessed are the merciful, for they shall be shown mercy.

8, Blessed are the pure in heart, for they will see God.

9, Blessed are the peacemakers, for they will be called the sons of God.

10, Blessed are those who are persecuted because of righteousness, for theirs is the kingdom of heaven.

11, Blessed are you when people insult you, persecute you and falsely say all kinds of evil against you because of me.

12, Rejoice and be glad, because great is your reward in heaven, for in the same way they persecuted the prophets who were before you.

~ Matthew 5

Meditate on
These Things

Whatever things are true,
Whatever things are noble,
Whatever things are just, Whatever
things are pure,
Whatever things are lovely,
Whatever things are of good report,
If there is any virtue and if there is anything
praiseworthy—Meditate/think on these things.
~ *Philippians 4:8*

"What you need to know about the past is that no matter what has happened, it has all worked together to bring you to this exact moment and time. You have to go through that, to get to this!"

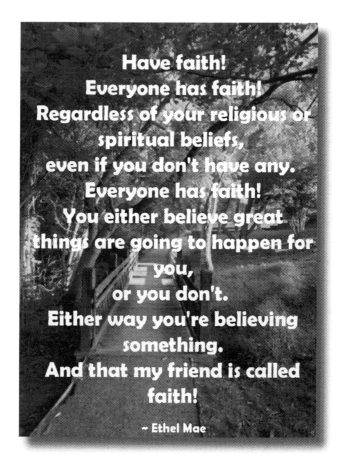

Have faith!
Everyone has faith!
Regardless of your religious or
spiritual beliefs,
even if you don't have any.
Everyone has faith!
You either believe great
things are going to happen for
you,
or you don't.
Either way you're believing
something.
And that my friend is called
faith!

~ Ethel Mae

The definition of faith: complete trust or confidence in someone or something.

As you are believing for something anyway (having faith), you might as well believe big, believe hard. Believe that great and amazing things will happen for and to you.

Walk over the bridge into your greatness, believe you can and believe it will be great once you get to the other side. Just don't forget to enjoy the journey.

Your Thoughts..........

Whatever you want to accomplish, you already have the tools to do so. Reach inside and pull out your confidence and faith.

YES, you've made mistakes. Life doesn't come with instructions. You are a work in progress... You'll fall, but you will get back up. . . .one step at a time... Take baby steps since Rome wasn't built in a day! Be thankful for life!

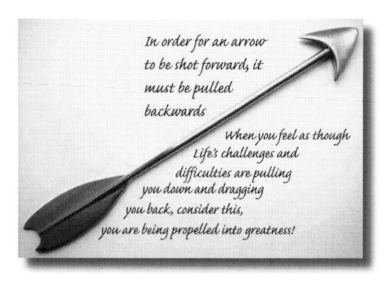

In order for an arrow
to be shot forward, it
must be pulled
backwards

When you feel as though
Life's challenges and
difficulties are pulling
you down and dragging
you back, consider this,
you are being propelled into greatness!

Choose to LOVE - Rather than HATE.
Choose to LAUGH - Rather than CRY.
Choose to CREATE - Rather than DESTROY.
Choose to PERSEVERE - Rather than QUIT.
Choose to PRAISE - Rather than GOSSIP.
Choose to HEAL - Rather than WOUND.
Choose to GIVE - Rather than STEAL.
Choose to ACT - Rather than PROCRASTINATE.
Choose to GROW - Rather than ROT.
Choose to PRAY - Rather than CURSE.
Choose to LIVE - Rather than DIE.
~Unknown-

Serve A Purpose

Does it serve any purpose to complain about things you cannot change? So why would you want to waste your time doing it?

Does it serve any purpose to fill your thoughts with regret & resentment over what happened long ago? So why would you waste even a single moment on such a negative and unpleasant pursuit?

You're better off doing something that does serve a purpose. You're better off using your time and energy to learn, to create, to love, to understand, and to experience the beauty of life.

Your thoughts & actions are immensely powerful. Rather than using them to hold weigh down, put them to work on a valuable and positive purpose.

Use your energy to serve your highest good, a positive purpose, and as a result, you will have more energy. Fill your time in the pursuit of a fulfilling and positive purpose and your life will be filled with truly meaningful treasures.

Choose the thoughts & actions that serve a purpose, and life will serve you its real rewards.

Don't Judge

Don't judge each day by the harvest you reap but by the seeds that you plant. So today, plant Hope, Peace, Harmony, Unconditional Love, Trust, and Respect, so that you will reap a brighter happier tomorrow filled with Hope, Peace, Harmony, Unconditional Love, Trust, and Respect. You never lose anything by giving love, you lose by holding back.

Love is the Most Important Thing

Love is the most important thing. It's not about how much you have, how much you know, who you know, or how much you do. It's about how well you love. Love is what matters the most.

Appreciate

You can wish for more but until you fully appreciate what you already have, it will be a struggle to manifest more.

It's not the amount that matters, but the blessings and lessons you are able to receive from it. A slice of stale bread gives more to the beggar, than a new house to the rich. Everything you have has unending blessings for you hidden inside, learn to receive them.

Back on Track

It's never too late to get back on track. Never has anyone gone so far on the wrong path that they cannot return to the right one. Never has anyone become so wayward that they cannot benefit from the true light.

You can break free from the prison of your past and no longer allow it to hold you captive. Learn from the experiences that took you off track, own your experiences, and grow from your experiences.

If inside, you possess good qualities, such as compassion or spiritual forgiveness, then external factors will not affect the internal peace of the mind.

Touch the Earth with your feet, lift your face to the sun, breathe the air, listen to the birds and the wind through the trees. Glory in the creation that surrounds you.

*"When babies take their first step and fall, we praise the first step, we
don't criticize the fall. We as adults could learn a lesson from this. We
spend more time criticizing and finding fault when we fall and not
enough time recognizing and appreciating our small steps forward"*

Everyone Reaps
What They Sow.....
Not So True

We've all heard the age-old adage, "you reap what you sow." But just suppose that is not exactly true.

Image this, an apple, and the size of an apple seed. When the apple seed is planted (sown), the seed will take years between 6 – 10 years for an apple tree to grow to maturity.

Once the tree has grown, it will produce hundreds of apples year, after year, after year. Generations after you will still be eating the fruit of the tree long after you are gone.

That is something to think about. Now change the apple tree into people. The life you are living today, is a result of the seeds you have sown years ago. Your experiences be they good or bad are the harvest for all you have 'planted'.

We all seen a movie where families have been fighting for generations. Eventually there comes a point down the line the families don't even know why they are fighting. But because their great, great, great grandfathers didn't speak, for whatever reason. Your families have been at war. The reason the fall out began may not even be important anymore. A prime example of future generations reaping the harvest sown years previously.

Be careful of what you sow because that is what you will reap and experience in your life and could affect the lives of those you love for years to come.

If you want good, do good, sow good seed, seeds of peace, love, kindness, forgiveness (there will come a time when we will need to forgive and be forgiven)

If you want bad, sow bad seeds, seeds of lies, distrust, deception, unforgiveness

Remember, you reap what you sow, well kinda!

Your Thoughts..........

_____

_____

_____

_____

_____

_____

_____

_____

_____

_____

_____

_____

_____

"The question to ask yourself
isn't who is going to let you:
the true question should be,
who is going to stop you?"

Whatever you have, hoped, dreamed and prayed for, don't allow the naysayers make you doubt yourself. Go ahead, write that book, buy that house, go back to school, change career, start that business, travel the world.

Keep going, keep building your dream, keep using your gifts and talents, the results may just astound you. So, the question is "who's going to stop you?"

The painful part about this is, many times, nobody else stops you but you. You allow the naysayers to get into your head, you allow self-doubt to block and hinder you, you allow the fear of failure to hold you back.

It is time to get out of your own way, push past all those who say it can't be done. Ignore those who make you feel bad for working hard to achieve your goals and build your dream. Because at the end of the day, if you are not building your dream, you are working at a job to build the dream of someone else.

It is time to get out of your own way and GO!!!!

Let it Go!!!

In the wise words of Queen Elsa from the Disney movie, *Frozen*,

"Let It Go".

"It's funny how some distance makes everything seem small And the fears that once controlled me can't get to me at all It's time to see what I can do To test the limits and break through"

What a message coming from a children's animated movie.

Or as James Bay puts it in his song "Let It Go"

Holding something we don't need.
This delusion in our heads.
Is gonna bring us to our knees.
It's funny how reflections change.
When we're becoming something else,
Trying to push this problem up the hill,
Think now's the time to let it slide,
So come on let it go, just let it be.

But let's really think about this for a minute. *"Holding something we don't need, all this delusion in our heads is gonna bring us to our knees"*

Baggage, baggage, baggage, baggage, and more baggage! All the pain, anger, regret, doubt, mistrust, fear, shame, guilt, and insecurities that are holding you back and keeping you stuck in the perpetual cycle of the past, **Let It Go!** The only place that all of these emotions are alive and well is in your head, the battle of your mind. As the saying goes, "get out of your own head."

Letting go of the baggage you carry around, be it emotional or mental is necessary to be able to move on, as what angers you and what you think of the most is what controls you. We don't forget the emotional or mental pain, but you can let it go, to live a better life.

Letting go isn't just about releasing the past, it is also having the knowledge, wisdom, and insight to embrace the present and future. It is looking forward to a better way of living and better place of being within. A place of peace.

So often, all of the things from the past that hurt you the most, the pain, anger, regret, doubt, mistrust, fear, shame, guilt, and insecurities is carried around like baggage. But guess what? You lived through it, you survived, you came through the other side albeit wounded and scarred, but you made it through. You can't undo the past or change anything that has happened. But you can stop it from living on in your mind, you can stop replaying the events, you can stop reliving it. You can and must release it and let it go!

Please hear me, I am not saying that it is going to be easy or that it will happen with just a click of your fingers or a click of your heels, or just by thinking good positive thoughts. But if you really and truly want to be a whole person with peace and contentment in your life, you must practice letting go of all the baggage that is hurting you and holding you back. And I do promise you this, it will be worth it.

Letting go means opening your mind and heart to looking ahead. How can you move forward if you are always looking in the rearview mirror? Pretty soon, you will end up in an accident if all you are doing is trying to drive a car forward while looking behind you all the time. Pay attention to what is ahead. Pay attention to the amazing possibilities that are right in front of you that mostly get over-

looked because you are busy caught up in your head, reliving and replaying what was done. Even sometimes, going as far as creating scenarios in our minds like a safety blanket to hold on to. Playing out scenes of revenge or getting even. But letting it go is a must, sometimes we have to let go of is what is killing us, even if it is killing us to let go!

I once saw a presentation where a man opened the trunk of his car and it was full to overflowing with stuff, just junk and stuff. He was then trying to put other things in there on top of all the stuff and junk that was already in there. He then realized that in order to get something new into the trunk he had to let go and clear out all of the stuff and junk that had been accumulated over time.

It is the same with your life, in order to fully embrace what is ahead and truly, fully live, you need to let go of all the hurt, pain, and dis-

appointments that held you back and in the past.

By not letting it all go what is it costing you?

The only time you are supposed to pay for excess baggage is when you are travelling! PERIOD! And sometimes not even then.

It is literally killing you, can you honestly say that holding on to all of the baggage makes you are happy? Holding onto baggage pushes people away. Who wants to be around all of that negativity? Who wants to be around a person that can't embrace a bright and hopeful future? Do you what to be around a person like that? So why be that person?

Letting go is not to say "right, that's it, I will forget and never again think of or remember what has been." Not at all! We shouldn't nor can we really forget the past, as there are also good times and happy memories, there were lessons that have been learnt from the past. Letting go is a necessity, it is releasing all the negative emotions associated with the past. By letting go, you open yourself up to experience new relationships, new ideas, new happiness, and a whole new and exciting life. Don't let the past ruin it for the future.

> *"It is time to unpack and put the bags away!*
> *It's time to put it down, isn't it too heavy now?"*

Here are some of the lyrics from the song Bag Lady released in 2000 by Erykah Badu, so you see, this is nothing new!

Bag lady you gone hurt your back.
Dragging all them bags like that.
One day all them bags gon' get in your way, so pack light.
Bag lady you gon' miss your bus.
You can't hurry up, you got too much stuff.
I know, sometimes it's hard and we can't let go.
If you start breathin' babe.
Bag lady let it go, let it go you.

Your Thoughts..........

_____

_____

_____

_____

_____

_____

_____

_____

_____

_____

_____

_____

_____

_____

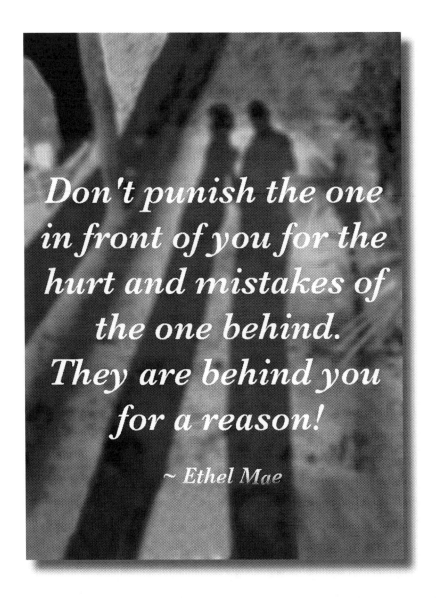

Don't punish the one
in front of you for the
hurt and mistakes of
the one behind.
They are behind you
for a reason!

~ Ethel Mae

Take Your Power Back!

Take your power back; what exactly does that mean? Take your power back, where exactly did it go? Imagine that you have a very valuable and precious box, and you have put your self-esteem, confidence, self-respect and 'power' into that box. The box also holds your purpose, your values, your sense of self, your boundaries, and of course, your 'power', along with other ideals that shape who you are. You should keep it close to you, after all, it is precious and filled with what makes you who you are.

But when you lack confidence and have low self-esteem and you begin to look for validation in all the wrong places, you feel as though the contents of your box in not enough. At some point in your life, you may have had enough of all of the items in your box. But life, relationships, work, etc. happened and you got to a stage where you no longer valued them as much. So, you take them out of the box and give them to people who are undeserving. You go through life with the box in your hands ready to hand it to the first person who is willing to take it. This way, you have shifted the responsibility onto another, leaving you powerless. It is as though you don't want the responsibility of yourself, of trusting your own judgement.

Eventually, when the person or thing goes, you are given your box back, only now it is all beat up. If it is a person that you had given your box to who keeps yo-yoing in and out of your life, they will still hold onto something as an entry point back in. When you are desperate to gain their validation and approval, you will keep taking them back believing that it is the only way to feel valued. And so the cycle continues.

You wonder how you will survive now that the things you didn't value and cherish are gone (the items in the box) and you feel helpless. You believe you are powerless.

Then, as though, out of nowhere, maybe after a traumatic experience with what/whoever you have given your power to, you have an aha moment. Usually, at a time when you have reached your limit, you come to the realization that what you had in the box is restorable, you can grow again you can heal and you are whole. The more you use your attributes in the box and nurture them, the more they grow.

You are not without power or control, you are however someone who doesn't seem to believe they deserve their own power. It is as though you do not see your qualities correctly. Someone can only have power over you if you have given it away and allow them to.

"For most people, they give up their power with the popular misconception, thinking they don't have any."

When you give your power away, the reality of what you are doing is taking the focus away from you and giving it to a person or a thing. Now, in order to be powerful, you need to have the ability to make choices that come from you, your resolve, your determination, and your spirit; not from another person. It needs to be you who will make choices to act or to make decisions based on your convictions and your beliefs and your will power. And that, my dear friends is having power.

There is an all-important question to ask yourself, do you have the ability to make choices that come from your will and to put them into actions if you wanted to? If the answer is no, then the real questions you have to ask yourself is, who has your power? Is it your partner, is it your job? Are you stopped by fear? Have you given your power to a religion or a philosophy? Have you given your power to controlling and domineering people, comfort foods, substances such as alcohol or drugs?

Are you a care giver, and has this left you feeling powerless? Or, do you let people who have a negative outlook drain you? Have you given your power away to money or time, or the lack of it?

A person doesn't necessarily need to say or do anything to take your power. When you let your mind wander and you spend your time imagining situations that have you as being helpless while someone else is in control and holds all the cards, it is you that is removing your power, not them. Stop imagining and focusing on negative situations, challenge and dismiss the negative images.

For you to step into your power, you must take your power back from those who have a distorted meaning of power and how to use it. You will need to take it back from all the people and things you have given it to. Forgive them and forgive yourself for giving your power away to them.

I have encountered people who, no matter what is said to them, have an answer and an excuse for everything that gives them a reason to stay powerless. They believe that all the power has been taken away from them by something or someone else. They never take responsibility for the fact that power is given away and very rarely taken away. If you continually put people on a pedestal, they'll only look at you from above, which puts you in a powerless position in being below them.

You are never powerless, you have choices at every point. You have even had the power to make choices to be powerless, a subconscious choice, but a choice none the less. Why not make a choice now to be powerful? Why not use your power to reclaim your self-esteem, your confidence, your strengths and your abilities?

You decide and determine your value in the same way that you decide and determine your power. If you don't value yourself, have values, and act accordingly, you are allowing people to treat you without value. Why should they treat you any other way than how they see you treat yourself, they are just following your lead! The power to change someone and force them to see your value and appreciate it in the way that you want to be seen and appreciated lies with you.

> *"You don't have to hide behind the victim mask anymore.*
> *Tear it off and take your power back!*
> *Take it back from everyone who has ever hurt you.*

You will surprise yourself.
You're stronger than you know."

Stop being and feeling like a victim. If you think like a victim, you will act like a victim and you will be a victim. In turn, you are rendering yourself powerless. Even if you have been treated badly or unfairly, holding onto a victim mentality is not an empowering one it doesn't serve you. Don't continue to romanticize negative thoughts and feelings, as you are only encouraging yourself to hold on to negative emotions and being powerless. Recognize and understand why you feel the way you do so you can take control of yourself and feel more empowered.

The power to feel change is yours. The power to feel happy and content is yours. You can point out the faults in others all you want, but that is just a waste of time, effort and energy. It will not change the reality of who they are or how you feel about yourself. You give away your power every time you decide that it is the responsibility of others to change. It is time to take responsibility for your happiness.

So, what are you waiting for, Take your Power Back! Why not start today?

Your Thoughts..........

All Pieces of the Same Puzzle

When things happen in life, it is often difficult to see the big picture. To see how everything is divinely orchestrated and connected. To see that everything is in fact "all pieces of the same puzzle."

Life can get us broken into pieces. We are left feeling fragmented. But in time, with love, consideration, concentration, tenderness, patience, and careful thought, things will get put together in the right order.

All pieces of the same puzzle

It is then that we will see that all along there was a bigger picture all throughout life. All of the pieces and components all serve a purpose and has a place.

God will put all the pieces of your life together. And you will be able to see the beautiful picture.

The pieces will make a beautiful unique picture, the picture of your life.

All pieces of the same puzzle!

What Would You Go Back in Time & Tell Your 4-Year-Old Self?

So, a few weeks ago, I found a picture of this ridiculously cute 4-year-old little girl. I looked at the picture of this cutie full of innocence, who had her whole life to unfold in front of her. And thought, if I could go back and speak to her, what would I tell her. I would tell her that life will have extreme highs, extreme lows, and LOTS in between.

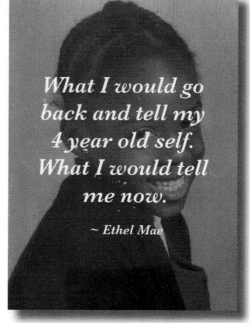

What I would go back and tell my 4 year old self. What I would tell me now.

~ Ethel Mae

I would tell her to remember to cherish the good times, but hold on tight during the difficult times because she will get through them.

I would tell her that she will make mistakes in life, learn from them, let them go, forgive herself, and move on, to just keep it moving.

I would tell her she will get hurt, she will have her heart broken, she will be lied to, lied about and used; I would tell her to forgive them, love them, and release them.

I would tell her that she will cry tears of immense pain, but she will also cry tears of extreme happiness and joy.

I would tell her that she is loved unconditionally by an AMAZING God who will never leave her and will keep every promise He has made to her.

I would tell her not to despise the dark days, as growth comes with sunshine *and* rain, it can't be sunny all the time and it will not rain all the time.

I would tell her to keep dreaming, keep believing, keep aiming high. To not allow anyone or anything to stifle her or steal her dreams or her joy or stifle her. I would tell her to keep moving, keep learning, keep growing, as nothing good comes from stagnation.

But most of all, I would tell her I love her even during the times that it feels as though no one else does. I would tell her it will be alright, everything will be alright, just have faith, trust, and believe. I would tell her that God is faithful. I would tell her she is BEAUTIFUL, and to never allow anyone to make her feel she is not.

I can't go back and speak to her, what I will do is tell her to take a look and really read everything written above as she enters into each new year. I will tell her to not just look at the words but really take them in, apply them, live them.

Little girl, Live, Dream, Believe, Pray, Hope, Laugh, Cry, and Love!

If you could, what would you go back and tell your 4-year-old self? Seeing that as you can't go back, starting today, what are you telling you?

Make life count from today onward!

Your Thoughts.........

_____

_____

_____

_____

_____

_____

_____

_____

_____

_____

_____

_____

_____

_____

Superman & Clark Kent

A few of years ago while going through a separation and divorce. I noticed a few social media posts attempting to belittle me. He decided that he didn't want to be with me, which is fine! Making the breakdown because I worked too much, I made him feel bad about himself, as I pushed him too hard to achieve *HIS* goals and it wasn't "fun" anymore. There was a reason for working so much. It was to achieve a goal we had set. Before we had split up, He started a relationship with another woman where they both thought humiliating and disrespecting me on social media was "keeping it classy."

I remember one particular post he put on Instagram that read, "she was so busy looking for Superman that she walked past Clark Kent every day." And true to form, the female he was with thought it was the right thing to do by commenting on *MY* then husband's post, taking shots at me. I chose to keep my dignity and stay silent. I am not perfect, as unfortunately, I did take the bait on an occasion and put up a post that said, "the best apology is changed behavior." As he would apologize when I confronted him with it, only to put something up within a few days.

Anyway, back to Clark Kent. I took the post very personally, reading it over and over again and agonizing and questioning myself every time I read it. Reading her comment fixated on the heart emojis she would use.

Once I made the decision to move past this, I got out of ALL my feelings (thank you Kiki).

I thought, "I challenge that BS! What is wrong with looking for Superman?" I thought, "what is wrong with me seeing greatness within my husband and wanting to pull it out of him? What is *wrong* with me wanting my husband to see what I see in him and supporting and encouraging him to be all he was destined to be? What is *wrong* with me wanting my husband to walk in his God given purpose? What is *wrong* with my not wanting my husband to settle for mediocrity? What is *wrong* with me wanting to draw his strength and potential to the surface and have him walk in his calling? What is *wrong* with all of that?"

What is *wrong* is when he is comfortable being Clark Kent. What is *wrong* is when he is content to stay running in circles.

What is *wrong* is when he has allowed fear to keep him in mediocrity.

What is *wrong* is when his purpose is so big that it scares him. What is *wrong* is that he cannot see, within himself, the strength and the potential that you as the woman in his life sees in him. What is *wrong* is when anyone, be it family, friends or another female will indulge and enable this behavior and make you the villain because you won't allow him to settle for less than who he can be. When you think of it, Clark Kent was not his true authentic self. That was the front, the mask he put on to fit in, to conform, to blend in.

What is *wrong* is when your strength and your drive scares him into thinking he doesn't and can't measure up. What is *wrong* is when your success makes him feel as though he is less of a man. As much as that is not what you are trying to or want to do.

Unfortunately, we are still in in an age where some men are not comfortable with women being more successful than they are. Now, there are those women that use their success and education to make their partners feel inadequate, but we are not referring to that demographic.

My dear sister, my dear Queen, you are right for looking for and seeing the Superman within him, whilst still honoring that he is currently Clark Kent. You are right for wanting to push him beyond his comfort zone. You are right for seeing the King in him. You are right for seeing his potential. You are right that you want him to see within himself what you see in him and know he can be. You are right for wanting to draw the Superman out of him. You are right that you do not want the labels that society has placed on our men to be his reality. You are right for wanting to challenge him.

You are right, you are right, YOU ARE RIGHT!

Don't be so hard on yourself, don't feel as though you are any less, because he chose the easy way. Don't second guess yourself, because he chose to settle in mediocrity. Pick yourself up, dust yourself down, shake it off. You deserve a King that will appreciate your confidence, support, and belief in him. One who will appreciate and respect you.

Believe that your King, your Superman, WILL find you! And when he does, he will appreciate you and love you all the more for being his biggest and best cheerleader. He will be the strong King that you need.

Your Thoughts.........

_____

_____

_____

_____

_____

_____

_____

_____

_____

_____

_____

_____

_____

Be Careful of The, "I Knew Them When" Kind of People

> *When bringing your vision to life and building your dream, surround yourself with people who have the same drive, values and ideas but different abillities and talents.*
>
> ~ Ethel Mae

I am sure we have all been a part of a conversation or heard a conversation with, "yeah, but I knew them when…." You can fill in the blank. We may even have been the person that has said it or been the subject of that conversation. History can't be rewritten, nor does that mean you have to be constantly reminded of it. Everyone has a past, and for some, there are parts that would much rather be forgotten. But the past is what has led you to this very moment, it has shaped your life. It is such a shame that when looking at your accomplishments, there is always one person that will say those six disparaging words, "Yeah, but I knew them when…" then will go on to list a string of past indiscretions, live and in living color!

We have all had our fair share of challenges and experiences in life, the good, the bad, the ugly and the indifferent. These experiences, once you have learnt the life lesson can serve as valuable insights and tools to help others and help you not repeat the same mistakes. If you were to reflect on those experiences and look at how far you have come, you will realize how life transforming they are. And be grateful for a more enlightened path you are now on and how your life has changed for the better.

If it hadn't it would give the naysayers nothing to talk about.

You have worked for all you have and for where you are in life and unfortunately there are some that do not want to see you succeed. They are happy for you as long as you are not doing better than they are. It may not even be that they dislike you per se, because people operate from a place of either love or fear. Sadly, more often than not they operate from a place of fear. Fear of change, things no longer being familiar and comfortable.

There are some people who are just downright mean spirted and very quick to judge. Those same people will try to define you based on who you were, not who you've become and who you are growing to be. They'll want you to stay stuck with them on memory lane and try to steal your momentum and drive. They will try to stop you from embracing your future. Don't let them! You need to move beyond the "good old days." The past is past; it can't be erased or rewritten, it can only be replayed and rehashed over and over. It is for you to write the rest of your story. The future lies before you and waiting to be explored.

Success will often reveal who is really for you and who is genuinely happy for you. So be careful of who you surround yourself with. Just as you can manifest your life with your thoughts and beliefs, the same can be said for who you surround yourself with, it affects what you ultimately believe and become.

Just as you should be mindful of who you surround yourself with, you also need to be careful who it is you take advice from. Guess what? Not everyone has your best interest at heart. Shocker! I know. But it is the truth. When seeking advice, speak to those who you would like to emulate, people who are where you want to be in life. And even then, don't take everything at face value, do your own research, use your own discernment.

True, good, genuine friends are hard to find, so when you find them, hold on to them and cherish them. Because no matter how much of a nice, hardworking, successful person you are, you will ultimately make enemies. That is just a natural part of life, so don't let it phase you. People see what it is they want to see, you could be the Archbishop they will still find fault and something to criticize.

The reality is, traits hated in you is what others actually hate about themselves and just project outward and vice versa. The good thing is that this is an opportunity for growth. Growth to express patience and understanding. Don't fear enemies, use them as your chance to show love and compassion, for you to rub off on them. As their animosity really is just their fears being expressed.

It brings to mind an expression from the Bible, "a prophet is without honor in his own hometown". Basically, some people that knew Jesus as a child from his hometown, when He returned teaching, they had no respect for the works that He performed. Their comments were "where did He get this wisdom? Isn't this the carpenter's son?" Basically, we knew him when.... What did Jesus do? He kept it moving, He left them behind. He didn't allow them to keep Him in His past, or stuck in a previous stage of life, or where he was from, or who his parents were nor did He allow it to define Him.

Don't stop living your life because you fear what others will say of your success. You can't let the "they've changed" or "they think they are too good for us now" or the "yeah, but I knew them when" let you stop reaching for and achieving greatness. Because what others think of you is none of your business. One of the most draining and restrictive fears that will hold you back from reaching your goals is the fear of what others might think of you.

The core of what holds many back in life is this fear, so it goes without saying that accepting this and overcoming it will change your life. Believe in yourself, develop self-belief this will help you to disregard the negative, disparaging noise.

There is no point in looking back in regret just because a few negative people choose to hold on to the past. Don't waste your time on their jealousy or let others make you think that you cannot or are not making a difference.

There will be times you're ahead, and times you're behind. The race of life is long, and, in the end, you should only be competing with yourself.

So, remember the compliments and forget the negative comments. Live in truth, your truth. Achieve and live in peace within yourself and those around you. Peace is what you should endeavor to have. It ultimately is what we all want.

Your Thoughts.........

The robbed that smiles steals something from the thief

— William Shakespeare

Pack your luggage light, baggage will only weigh you down!

Pack Light!

About the Author

Ethel Mae, a survivor of childhood physical and sexual abuse, was an angry and often lonely teenager who suffered mental and sexual abuse as an adult. She has always had a drive to prove those that wanted to see her fail wrong. She was able to turn her life around through hard work and faith. She is a mentor to teens, a life coach, writes for magazines, and is an author. She is also the author of *Broken Pieces Behind The Mask.*

Printed in the United States
By Bookmasters